T0198496

*The Third Karmapa's Mahamudra Prayer*

# The Third Karmapa's Mahamudra Prayer

*by*
The XII Khentin Tai Situpa

*translated and edited by*
Rosemarie Fuchs

Snow Lion
Boulder

Snow Lion
An imprint of Shambhala Publications, Inc.
4720 Walnut Street
Boulder, Colorado 80301
www.shambhala.com

© 2002 by Tai Situpa and Rosemarie Fuchs

Printed in the United States of America

⊗This edition is printed on acid-free paper that meets the
American National Standards Institute Z39.48 Standard.
♻Shambhala Publications makes every effort to print on recycled
paper. For more information please visit www.shambhala.com.
Snow Lion is distributed worldwide by Penguin Random House,
Inc., and its subsidiaries.

*Library of Congress Cataloging-in-Publication Data*
Pema Donyo Nyinche, Tai Situpa XII, 1954–
The Third Karmapa's Mahamudra prayer / [commentary by] the
XII Khentin Tai Situpa; translated and edited by Rosemarie Fuchs.
p. cm.
ISBN 9781559391696 (alk. paper)
1. Raṅ-byuṅ-rdo-rje, Karma-pa III, 1284–1339. Ṅes don phyag rgya
chen po'i smon lam. 2. Māhāmudra (Tantric rite). 3. Meditation—
Bka'-rgyud-pa (Sect). 4. Bka'-rgyud-pa (Sect)—Rituals. I. Fuchs,
Rosemarie, 1950– . II. Raṅ-byuṅ-rdo-rje, Karma-pa III, 1284–1339.
Ṅes don phyag rgya chen po'i smon lam. III. Title.
BQ7682.6.R363 P46 2001
294.3'443—dc21
2001006593

# Contents

## Translator's Note

In November 1994 the XII Khentin Tai Situpa kindly accepted an invitation by Chime Rinpoche, the spiritual head of the German Buddhist center Kagyu Benchen Ling, located in Todtmoos-Au, Black Forest, to give teachings on the Mahamudra prayer composed by the Third Gyalwa Karmapa. He gave his permission for these oral teachings to be rendered into writing, and authorized the version presented here. He also showed the great kindness of examining and correcting the editor's translation of the prayer itself, which is included herein. To Caitlin Collins, Alexander Wilding, and Lama Alasdair MacGeagh I would like to express my gratitude for their proofreading and corrections. I am thankful to Snow Lion Publications for making this teaching available to interested readers and to Chris Hatchell for his careful editing of my English.

Rosemarie Fuchs

Hamburg, February 10th, 1996

# About the Tai Situpa

The Khentin Tai Situpa, Pema Dönyö Nyingjé Wangpo,
is the twelfth incarnation of the Tai Situpa lineage. The
Tai Situpas are one of the most important lineages of the
Kagyü tradition, and play a significant role in maintain-
ing the continuity of the teachings. The members of this
lineage are regarded as emanations of the future Buddha
Maitreya, who currently resides in Tushita until the time
comes for him to incarnate upon earth. The Situpa line,
before being so named, is said to have begun with Lotsawa
Marpa of Lodrak, the disciple of Naropa and master of
Milarepa; next came Drogön Rechen, one of the heart sons
of Düsum Khyenpa, the First Gyalwa Karmapa; he was
followed by Naljor Yeshe Wangpo and Rigowa
Ratnabhadra. The line is closely associated with Guru
Rinpoche, and is referred to in his predictions.

The present Tai Situpa was born in 1954 at Taiyul, Tibet, in accordance with the predictions of the Sixteenth

Gyalwa Karmapa, who enthroned him at Palpung. On the instructions of His Holiness, he left Tibet for Bhutan, prior to the Chinese invasion, and then proceeded to Rumtek, the seat of the Karmapa in Sikkim, where he received his education. At the age of twenty-two, he moved to Sherab Ling, near Dharamsala in Himachal Pradesh, to establish the monastery that is his principal seat outside Tibet. He has also founded the Maitreya Institute in Hawaii, and initiated the World Peace Movement, which aims at promoting intercultural and interfaith activity. Before the Sixteenth Karmapa passed away, he appointed the Tai Situpa as one of four regents charged with preserving the teachings of the Karma Kagyü lineage. As the principal holder of this lineage, having been given the complete transmission by the Sixteenth Karmapa, he will be responsible for passing these precious teachings on to the Seventeenth Gyalwa Karmapa, Urgyen Thrinlé Dorjé.

The Tai Situpa is honored and respected by Buddhists throughout the world for his peerless ability to teach the Dharma both in the East and the West. His deep understanding of Western art and culture, especially of the Western psychological perspective, allows him to expound the Dharma with a clarity and directness that is truly inspiring. Those fortunate enough to have met him, or attended his teachings, will affirm his wisdom and compassion to be a constant source of inspiration.

*The Third Karmapa's Mahamudra Prayer:*
*Supplication for the Realization of Mahamudra*

# The Third Karmapa's Mahamudra Prayer: Supplication for the Realization of Mahamudra

*by the Third Gyalwa Karmapa, Rangjung Dorjé*

Namo Guru

Lamas, yidams, deities of the mandala, and victorious ones
Of the ten directions and three times together with your
    sons,
Please consider me with kindness and grant your blessing.
May it become conducive to my supplications being
    fulfilled as they are.

May the streams of the accumulation of virtue rise from
    the snow-mountain
Of the pure intention and action of myself and all beings
    limitless in number.
May these streams be free from the cloudiness of the three
    wheels
And thus flow into the ocean of the four kayas of the
    Victorious One.

As long as this is not attained, in all our future lifetimes,
Birth upon birth, may not even the sound
Of evildoing and suffering be heard.
May we enjoy the glory of an ocean of virtue and happiness.

Having attained supreme leisure and endowment,
  possessing faith, diligence, and wisdom,
Having relied on a good spiritual friend and received the
  essence of his instructions,
May we practice them properly without any hindrance,
And thus enact the sacred Dharma in all our future lives.

Through studying the words of the Buddha and the
  treatises of logic, we are freed from the veil of unknowing.
Through reflecting upon the oral instructions, we overcome
  the darkness of doubt.
Through the light born from meditation, the true nature
  shines forth as it is.
May the brilliance of the three wisdoms spread.

The two truths which are free from the extremes of
  eternalism and nihilism are the meaning of the ground.
Through the supreme path of the two accumulations,
  which is free from the extremes of assertion and denial,
We attain the fruit, the twofold benefit, which is free from
  the extremes of existence and mere peace.
May we meet this Dharma, unmistaken and free from error.

The ground to be purified is the mind itself, the union of
  clarity and emptiness.
The means of purification is the great vajra-yoga of
  Mahamudra.
What is to be removed are the adventitious stains of delusion.
The fruit of purification is the dharmakaya free from stains.
  Through these means may it reveal itself directly.

Cutting our doubts with regard to the ground brings
   conviction of the view.
Preserving this without distraction is the essence of
   meditation.
Skillfully enacting the meaning of meditation in everything
   is supreme conduct.
May we gain certainty in the view, meditation, and conduct.

All phenomena are illusory manifestations of our mind.
As for the mind, there is no mind: it is empty of essence.
It is empty and yet unceasingly appears everywhere.
Investigating well, may we discern the fundamental root.

Self-appearance which never existed is mistaken for an
   object.
Under the domination of ignorance, self-awareness is
   mistaken for a self.
By the power of dualistic fixation we wander through the
   realm of existence.
May we eradicate our ignorant delusion.

It is not existent, since even the Victorious One does not
   see it.
It is not non-existent, since it is the basis of everything, of
   samsara and nirvana.
These not being contradictory, it is unity, the path of the
   middle.
May we realize the true state of our mind, which is free
   from any extreme.

There is no way to illustrate it, saying "it is this."
There is no way to refute it, saying "it is not this."
The true state is beyond intellect, it is uncreated.
May the ultimate true meaning be confirmed.

As long as this is not realized, we circle in the ocean of
samsara.
Once it is realized, buddha is nowhere else.
Every [notion of] "it is this" or "it is not this" has fallen away.
May we be aware of the true state, the hidden secret of
our basis-consciousness.

Appearance is mind and emptiness is mind.
Realization is mind and delusion is mind.
Arising is mind and cessation is also mind.
Therefore, cutting all doubts, may we confirm everything
as mind.

Not adulterated by a meditation bound up with conceptual
strife,
And unmoved by the wind of ordinary bustle,
May we know how to abide naturally at ease in our
uncontrived innermost nature.
May we become skilled in this practice of the meaning of
mind, and maintain it.

The waves of gross and subtle thoughts subside in their
own place.
The stream of mind rests unmoved in itself.
May we be free from the stains of agitation, stupor, and
dullness,
And establish a still ocean of calm abiding.

While looking again and again at the mind which cannot
be looked at,
The meaning which cannot be seen is seen vividly, just as it is.
This cuts all doubts as to "this" and "not this" with regard
to the meaning.
May we be free from delusion and thus recognize our own
face.

When looking at an object, there is no object: it is seen as
  mind.
When looking at the mind, there is no mind: it is empty of
  essence.
When looking at both, dualistic fixation is freed of itself.
May we realize clear light, the nature of our mind.

Free from mental creation it is Mahamudra.
Free from extremes it is Great Madhyamaka.
Being all-inclusive it is also called Great Perfection.
May we gain certainty that, by knowing one, all meanings
  are realized.

Uninterrupted great bliss free from attachment,
Unobscured clear light free from fixation on characteristics,
Spontaneous absence of thought beyond intellect:
May these be experienced unceasingly without deliberate
  effort.

May our desire for good meditation, our clinging to
  experience, be liberated in its own place.
May the delusion of negative thoughts become pure as
  the expanse of the nature [of mind].
The ordinary mind is not to be obtained. There is nothing
  to be adopted and nothing to be abandoned.
May we realize the truth of the dharmata, which is free
  from any conceptual elaboration.

The nature of beings is always buddha.
Yet, not realizing this, they wander through the endless
  cycle of existence.
For all beings in their boundless suffering
May intolerable compassion be born in our stream of being.

Even as the skillful activity of intolerable compassion
    unfolds without hindrance,
May the meaning of its empty essence at the same time
    nakedly shine forth.
Inseparable from this supreme unerring path of union,
May we meditate at all times, day and night.

Developing the eyes and clairvoyant perception that arise
    from the power of meditation,
May we ripen beings, purify buddha-fields, and perfect
    the wishing prayers
That accomplish all the qualities of the Buddha.
May we lead the three aspects of perfecting, ripening, and
    purifying to their ultimate level and attain buddhahood.

By the power of the compassion of the victorious ones of
    the ten directions and their sons,
And by the power of every unstained virtue as much as
    there is,
May these pure supplications of myself and all beings
Reach fulfillment just as they are.

*Commentary by the XII Khentin Tai Situpa*

# Preliminary Remarks

This particular Mahamudra prayer, the most important points of which will be explained here, was written by the Third Gyalwa Karmapa, Rangjung Dorjé. There is a very comprehensive commentary to it, composed by the Eighth Tai Situpa, Chökyi Jungné. In the following, I will share whatever I know of this text and commentary, though I cannot go into too much detail due to the shortness of the time available.

Mahamudra is inclusive in that it covers everything involved in our lives, specifically in connection with the Vajrayana aspect of Lord Buddha's teaching. There are many ways to learn about Mahamudra—it can be taught through philosophical explanation or through meditation instruction. This particular teaching is in the form of a prayer. For me personally it is quite an interesting coincidence to have been requested to explain this particular prayer, since it has been an especially important inspiration to my work and practice. Therefore I hope you will draw something from it, and that it becomes just as useful to you as it is to me.

To begin with, it is extremely important to recall the definition of Mahamudra, and to know the sources of Mahamudra teaching itself. This is vital if we are to be able to relate to this subject.

### DEFINITION OF MAHAMUDRA

If Mahamudra is described in an academic way, it can become quite lengthy and complicated, to the point where it is almost no longer Mahamudra. I am not suggesting that there is no value in academic studies. I am quite academic myself in many ways, but I try to refrain from such an approach as far as this subject is concerned. The simplest way to understand the definition of Mahamudra is as follows. In its ultimate essence everything is perfect. Every sentient being is perfect. Every situation, every condition is perfect. That which is truly positive is ultimate. Perfection is ultimate. Freedom is ultimate. Liberation is ultimate. Therefore the ultimate truth is beyond any limitation; every single manifestation, no matter how good or bad it may be, is just the manifestation of this one limitless ultimate truth. It cannot be called "one," but this is better than saying "two." If it was "one," it would be limited. Concerning this point, many Mahamudra masters have stated: "I cannot say anything." Not to say anything would be the correct way of expression, as any word will not be quite accurate. Nevertheless, to describe it in the simplest and most direct way one can say: "Every relative manifestation is ultimately perfect." This is the essence of the highest form of Lord Buddha's teaching. At the same time it covers his most basic, fundamental teachings as well. Thus it covers everything. This is the definition of "Maha," which means "great."

There is a danger of misinterpreting and misunderstanding Mahamudra in a very fundamental way; the higher one flies, the harder one can fall. The Mahamudra teaching and principle are profound, and when understood rightly they are wonderful and very deep, but if we misunderstand them this will be a truly detrimental misunderstanding. In this respect a teacher will feel responsible.

When looking at sentient beings from the Mahamudra point of view, the basic attitude, which in a more formal way is also called "the view," is as follows. Every sentient being is equal to the Buddha. If amoebas have a mind, which I do not know, they are buddhas. Mosquitoes and flies definitely have a mind, so they are equal to the Buddha. Every single human being, every single animal, every single spirit, everything that has a mind, is equal to the Buddha. This is the Mahamudra view. Yet, even though beings are equal to the Buddha, this is on the ultimate level. On the relative level there is a difference. The Buddha is already enlightened, while sentient beings are not yet enlightened. The definition of "buddha" is enlightenment. The Tibetan word for "buddha" is *sang gyé*, which means "awakened and expanded." This is explained as "awakened from the sleep of ignorance and expanded in the direct vision of the whole range of the knowable." This is how we start looking at beings.

Then, within this perspective, how do we feel toward a sentient being who does not know that he or she is a buddha in potential? We feel compassion for them. In this way we respect sentient beings who are less enlightened than ourselves, while toward those who are more enlightened, we feel devotion. Thus we learn from those who are more enlightened and teach those who are less enlightened. We help and receive help. This is the relative truth from the Mahamudra point of view. In light of this relative truth there is a big difference between buddhas and sentient beings; at the same time, in light of the ultimate truth, there is no difference whatsoever. If we misunderstand this, we will have a big problem: we might consider ourselves better than the Buddha and think we can just do anything we like; if that happens we are definitely not yet enlightened and subject to a truly detrimental misconception. Whereas, if we understand it rightly, this is perfect, since our compassion for sentient beings will not lead us to think poorly about them. It will not cause a division between ourselves and sentient beings, a further separation. It will prevent us from having any notions that make such a dualistic difference between what we have and are able to do, as opposed to what they do not have and are not capable of doing. Our stomachs are full and their stomachs are empty. So we feel pity for them. But maybe their hearts are full and our hearts are empty. Thus, when understood rightly, compassion from the Mahamudra point of view is very deep, more profound than our ordinary concept of it.

So this does not mean that we do not have to respect the Buddha, and it does not mean that we do not have to care for sentient beings. We have to respect the Buddha until we have become a buddha ourselves, and we have to care for and help sentient beings until they have reached buddhahood. It is very important to be able to comprehend and deal with this kind of paradox.

Paradoxes can be said to be one of the most common features of Vajrayana teachings; this is especially true in teachings on Mahamudra. In this context it is inevitable that everything appears and is presented in a paradoxical way. There is the relative truth, which is an undeniable fact, being right here in front of our eyes. And there is the ultimate truth, that which this relative truth really is. As long as we cannot bridge this paradox, Vajrayana Buddhism is an impossible issue. Once we have gained this capacity, we will be able to understand the Vajrayana teachings and to appreciate the actual meaning behind them. One example of this kind of paradox is given in the

advice and instruction for practice; it is said: if we practice
the Vajrayana, and the Mahamudra in particular, our view
can be as vast as space while our actions must be as refined
as a speck of powder. This is the way in which practice
progresses. We know that in the ultimate sense there is
no such thing as good or bad, but as long as there is a self,
as long as we grasp ourselves as an "I," negative is negative and positive is positive. If we plant a potato and expect a tomato to grow, we will be really disappointed—we
might wait ten years and still be harvesting potatoes without seeing one single tomato. Yet whenever we decide to
respect the truth of relative reality, that tomato yields tomato and potato yields potato, once we accept this simple
fact, there will be no disappointment. So there is no way
to do negative things and expect good things to come out
of them, though ultimately they are the same. Ultimately
buddhas and sentient beings are the same, and hell and
heaven are the same, but this is not true on the relative
level. As long as we are given something nice and this
makes us happy, and we are hit and that hurts, good is
good and bad is bad.

In this way, the paradoxical aspect is reality. It is neither a conflict nor a problem, it is the truth. Thus the
practice of the Dharma means that throughout the whole
journey, until realization is reached, our view and our
action have to build a bridge between these two extreme
edges of the paradox. And the higher the teaching we

receive, the sharper the paradox will become, because as soon as the ultimate truth is presented there will be quite a contrast. As long as an instruction refers solely to the relative truth, there is no paradox to worry about. On this level, one talks in light of the Vinaya, in terms of rules such as "Do not steal," "Do not lie," and so forth, since these are negative actions. In this context there is no mention of the fact that ultimately they are neither good nor bad, and as long as this aspect is left aside, there is no need for the ability to comprehend paradoxes. Yet as soon as the ultimate teachings, such as those of the Vajrayana, are presented, paradox comes into play since we did not become enlightened just by hearing them—we merely heard and intellectually understood these teachings but have remained the same human beings with the same defilements. Nothing has changed except for having gained a greater understanding.

So when it is stated that these teachings are meant for highly intelligent people, this is not meant to belittle those who are not capable of practicing them. It means that a person must be able to comprehend, to have greater, further, and deeper understanding, and at the same time must control his or her ego without getting hazy. We need the ability to see reality clearly and to handle whatever we know. One can say that a person with this capacity is more mature and of greater intelligence, but besides this there is no difference between human beings.

There are people who are able to understand but then cannot deal with the understanding they gain. Conveying the Vajrayana teachings to such a person would be like giving an eight-year-old the opportunity of flying a 747. What would happen? He would come down in a crash with everybody else.

This is what we mean by saying that while the view can be as vast as space, still the action has to be as refined as a speck of powder. This aspect is very important.

I mention this in so much detail since I am teaching on Mahamudra and I do not want my words to cause anybody to walk out and think: "Everything is the same. Everything is all right and I am already a buddha." There is nothing wrong with that—it is a wonderful thought. But sooner or later, one will realize that one is not yet a buddha. And I would be responsible for everything that happened between these two events! I may be overemphasizing this point, but I hold it to be my duty. And I do not need any bad karma to keep me in samsara. Each of us has enough of that; we all have our share that we are trying to work out satisfactorily. So my words should also not lead anyone to think that he or she is a horrible person.

I am quite interested in the opportunities for practice provided by our modern era. Guru Rinpoche as well as Lord Buddha himself have mentioned in their prophecies that human beings during the time of degeneration will be increasingly more receptive to Vajrayana teaching and practice. With the little, almost non-existent wisdom I have, I can see the truth of these statements. In my personal view this is due to the degree of education and improved means of communication in modern times. Nowadays people are able to understand greater and deeper things far more easily than a hundred, two hundred, or three hundred years ago. In those days people were not exposed to so many ways of thinking and of relating to things as we are nowadays. This leads me to feel very good about our time. So I am not suggesting that we will make a lot of mistakes. Yet we need to understand that the emotions and defilements of human beings have not changed; in ancient times they were the same as they are nowadays. Whatever it took Milarepa to become enlightened, it will take us too. If we think we will become enlightened by taking a nice warm bath every day, watching television, going to different restaurants, and enjoying our life, this is a ridiculous notion. Whatever time span was necessary for Milarepa to attain enlightenment will be the very time span necessary for us, provided our karma is highly evolved enough to allow us to perform the things that such a great being was able to do; in this respect there is not the slightest difference.

So I do not think Guru Rinpoche's prophecy means to say that people in this time of degeneration will attain enlightenment faster or more easily. The teachings state very clearly, though, that human beings of this time will be appropriate vessels (Tib. *nö du rung wa*) for Vajrayana teachings. For me this term means receptive, having the capacity to easily understand and practice. Due to our intellectual improvement through the educational system and other means, we are able to understand complex things, and therefore maybe even paradoxes, much more easily. In this respect I am quite inspired to be born in our time. When I teach the Dharma in different countries and talk about this kind of subject, it is encouraging to see that there is an immediate response. I can read from the faces that there is at least a rough understanding of what this particular teaching is supposed to mean. This is an encouragement. It would be very difficult for me to relate anything if the audience just opened their eyes wide and showed no response! After some time I might think there was something wrong with me. This would be a big problem; I would not be able to communicate anything. So there is no need to worry; I am not worried either, just trying to be responsible.

As for calling our era a "time of degeneration," I believe in the reality of this in a particular way. There must be a much deeper meaning to it, yet in my simple understanding, I think it means that the good things are degenerating nowadays. In the early days of human history it may have been just as difficult to come across goodness as it is now, but at the same time it was very difficult to come across so many things that would attract our attention to such a great extent. When we examine the teachings of the Dharma very carefully, we find that the purpose of practicing is to realize what kind of inner potential each of us has. The real solution does not come from outside, it comes from us; it is within us. We are buddha, so all we have to do is to let this buddha manifest. This will not happen just by doing whatever comes to mind. If this were the case, birds and dogs would be enlightened long before human beings. They are much more free than we are. They do not have a lot of belongings and concepts, they do not learn the ABCs as we do, and they do not wear clothes. In this way they would be enlightened first and we would be left behind, which is not the case.

The real inner essence of each of us is buddha. When we meditate, the one simple thing that is happening is that all our dualistic concepts and the defilements which are their product are temporarily quieted down. Due to this, our essence, our mind which is buddha, has the opportunity to manifest a little bit. In this way we feel calm, we feel happy and clear, and we are able to see things more clearly—temporarily, of course. During the old days, opportunities to attract one's attention to the outside and to pamper one's senses were not abundant. One had to work extremely hard. In order to get drunk, for instance, one had to have a piece of land, and then one had to plant the wheat, wait for several months, and then cut it; the rain had to be in season and all the necessary conditions had to be favorable. Moreover, one had to know how to produce whiskey or beer, a process that took a lot of energy and time. Then one might have been unlucky and produced a very bad result, with the effect that one could not get drunk for another year. In this way gratifications of the senses were not abundant, whereas nowadays there are all kinds of things that hook us. We are like fish, and there are millions and millions of attractions, each of which can catch us and take us toward the outside. Thus there is abundance nowadays, in that it is extremely easy to find the means to corrupt our senses, our view, and our attitude. At the same time the means to overcome this, to look inside and let our buddha nature manifest, are just as rare as before, if not rarer.

That is in my view the definition of degeneration. It does not mean that there is something wrong with our time as such. I am sure that a long time ago the earth went around the sun with the same speed as it does now. I do not think that it has become faster or slower. Thus time is the same. Degeneration is defined by other things. On a superficial level the quality of life is better, while on a deeper level it has become so much worse. Due to this, family life is also degenerating. There is trouble between parents and children, trouble between couples, and trouble between different countries. Though, as far as countries are concerned, there was probably always trouble, ever since they existed; I think they exist because there was trouble beforehand, otherwise there would be no need for them! Yet on top of this there are all those new things which cause people to have so much trouble within themselves, and which will affect individuals' emotional health to a very great extent.

This is how I understand degeneration. At the same time, though, like a knife having been sharpened, our senses have become quite sharp nowadays, so if we gain the strength, if we have true awareness and a bit of wisdom, we can cut through things much more effectively than the people before us. In this respect I cannot help believing that people like us will be able to go deep and overcome a lot when we manage to make a firm resolve toward serious and proper practice. Worldly things are so abundant that for many people they are no longer exciting; having lost our excitement we can really say good-bye to them all, once we make the decision.

THE SOURCES OF MAHAMUDRA TEACHING

There are three major sources of all Mahamudra teachings. The first is the tantras (Tib. *gyü*). The second is all the texts written by the great Indian masters (Tib. *gya shung*). The third is the sacred oral instructions passed down from master to disciple (Tib. *men ngag*).

1. Generally speaking, Mahamudra is the essence of all the teachings of the Buddha. This particular method was taught by the Buddha in the highest form of tantra, in

which the Buddha himself manifests as a deity and his environment manifests as the surrounding of this deity. These two aspects form a mandala. The literal meaning of the term "mandala" is "center and surrounding": the center is the deity and the surrounding is the environment of the deity. This is considered to be a manifestation of the sambhogakaya, such as Kalachakra, Hevajra, Chakrasamvara, Guhyasamaja, Mahamaya, and so forth. Manifesting in this way the Buddha taught the highest of the four classes of tantras. In this context, the term "highest" should not be understood in the sense of hierarchy, such as "Captain Tantra," but in the sense of deepest, since these tantras represent the most profound aspect, the ultimate teaching of the Buddha. These are the actual and direct sources of all Mahamudra teachings.

2. *Gya shung* comprises all the scriptures that were written by Indian masters and later translated into the Tibetan language. These are instructions taught, for instance, by Nagarjuna, by the eighty-four mahasiddhas, by the thirty great female siddhas, and so forth.

3. As far as the third source, *men ngag,* is concerned, the teachings contained therein are limitless, since they depend upon the sincerity of the disciple in terms of his or her devotion and motivation, and depend upon the master's realization, as well as on his compassion, devotion, and so forth. In this way the instructions pertaining to *men ngag* have been passed all the way from the Buddha until now and will be continued as long as there is something to continue from.

The Mahamudra prayer by the Third Karmapa is also a certain type of *men ngag*. In the strict sense, *men ngag* depends entirely upon the individual—these instructions are given according to an individual's shortcomings and level of maturation. In this context, the practice appropriate for one individual might be the very practice inappropriate for another. Thus these teachings cannot be fixed in terms of one-sided ways and means. Each practitioner has his or her own aptitude and weaknesses, and the purpose of practice is to remedy the weaknesses and to make the aptitude mature. For this reason, *men ngag* has no limitation.

LINEAGE

I received the teachings on this prayer from several masters. The transmission was bestowed by His Holiness the Sixteenth Karmapa, while the teachings on the commentary were given by the Venerable Thrangu Rinpoche; I also received very essential instructions from the Venerable Salje Rinpoche. These I consider to be the source of the particular teaching that I am conveying to you; besides this there is influence from many Mahamudra and related practices, as well as from texts composed by other masters such as the Venerable Kalu Rinpoche.

CONCERNING THE TABLE OF CONTENTS

A very important feature of Tibetan Buddhist writing is the table of contents (Tib. *sab ché*). The table of contents creates a structure, so that a text flows from beginning to end. There is not a little bit here and a little bit there: the whole instruction is presented in a step-by-step process that definitely starts somewhere and ends somewhere else. The text presented here has basically three parts, the second of which in its turn divides into further subparts.

The first of the three main parts is the beginning of the prayer. This particular prayer is a supplication or *mön lam*, "a path of aspiration and longing." Therefore, at the beginning it is made clear who is praying to whom, and for what purpose. The second part is the actual prayer itself, the main part of the text; the last part is the conclusion of the prayer, the dedication. Any Mahayana or Vajrayana prayer or instruction divides into these three parts; they are called "the three sacred aspects," since they make the prayer or practice complete. If it were not for this structure, one might talk or write without beginning or end, and thus just produce gossip. The subject being holy, it would be holy gossip, but nevertheless, gossip! So at the beginning the purpose is presented very clearly, in the middle the deep teaching itself is conveyed, and at the end stands the dedication as a profound conclusion. In this way, the teaching is truly complete.

## Part One: Homage and Aspiration

The preliminary part of the Mahamudra prayer consists of these lines:

**Namo Guru**

**Lamas, yidams, deities of the mandala, and victorious ones
Of the ten directions and three times together with your sons,
Please consider me with kindness and grant your blessing.
May it become conducive to my supplications being fulfilled as they are.**

The Karmapa starts his prayer with the Sanskrit phrase "Namo Guru." Many Tibetan masters, whenever composing a text, use Sanskrit in the beginning, and sometimes also at the end, as a sign of their strong appreciation of and respect for the sources. It would have been easy for the Third Karmapa to translate "Namo Guru" into Tibetan (*lama la chag tsel lo*), but he used Sanskrit since our teachings originate from India and were translated from this language. The Karmapa's use of Sanskrit is a way of remembering and acknowledging the sources, the background, and the lineage. Though the prayer was composed in Tibetan, Sanskrit was used for these most important words: "Namo Guru," meaning, "I bow down to the Guru," or "Homage to the Guru."

The Karmapa then continues his prayer in Tibetan. He addresses all the lamas, yidams, and deities of the mandala, and then the buddhas of the ten directions and three times together with their sons, these latter being the bodhisattvas. He asks for their compassionate attention, and requests their blessing that whatever supplications he will utter may be fulfilled.

1. When speaking of the "lamas," one has to understand the definition of this term. There are four kinds of lama: the lineage lama, the root lama, the lama of blessing, and the lama in general. As for the literal meaning of the term "lama," *la* means "above" or "beyond," and *ma* means "mother." Thus a lama is someone who is above all sentient beings, and who cares for them just like a mother.

a. The lineage lama is to be understood as follows: every teaching we study or practice has to come from an unbroken lineage that stretches from the Buddha until now. It must have been handed on by one master to a disciple and by this disciple, having become a master himself, to the next disciple, and so forth; this process has to have continued uninterruptedly throughout two thousand five hundred years of Buddhist history. If this is not the case, the lineage is considered to be broken, and then it is no longer the authentic teaching of Lord Buddha, but is somebody else's interpretation. As long as the lineage is uninterrupted, its teaching contains blessing. This is what we study and practice; we do not study or practice somebody's interpretation of Lord Buddha's teaching. All the masters who are involved in this unbroken transmission of the Buddha's authentic teaching are called the lineage lamas.

According to tradition, one is not even allowed to read a Buddhist text without having received the proper transmission, but this aspect is often overlooked nowadays—increasingly we read anything. Nevertheless, an instruction for practice or a teaching that one intends to transmit cannot be derived from such sources: we cannot practice or teach anything unless this particular instruction has been transmitted properly. This is a very serious point within the Karma Kagyü lineage, as well as in the other lineages. When I was very young and had just come from Tibet to India, our attitude had not yet changed so much, and I was therefore not allowed, for instance, to open a book that contained tantric drawings of specific exercises or even of the nadis and chakras, since I had not completed the three years' retreat at that time. I was told I would go blind if I looked at such things! This may not be true in the literal sense, but still the lineage may be affected if anybody looks at these things and then tries to play with them. This should be taken into consideration, though nowadays, of course, tantric subjects are printed everywhere and sold in bookshops. One can even find mandalas on calendars! I am somewhat unhappy about this development, but what to do about it? Everybody has the freedom to do what he or she likes. But in my view this is a type of degeneration; it is definitely not an improvement.

b. The root lama in the actual sense is the teacher who introduces us to the recognition of our own buddha nature. Until this happens, the lama whom we consider to be our main teacher is our root guru. In the actual sense, Tilopa did not become Naropa's root guru until he had hit Naropa's cheek with his shoe—at that point Naropa fainted, and upon regaining consciousness found that he was enlightened. Marpa became Milarepa's root guru when his instructions had led Milarepa to recognize his buddha nature and thus reach enlightenment. Nevertheless, the moment that Naropa chose Tilopa to be his teacher and followed him everywhere, Tilopa became Naropa's guru; likewise, when Milarepa was searching for Marpa and, encountering a corpulent farmer ploughing a field with his oxen, asked: "Where is Marpa?" this first meeting was the moment when Marpa became Milarepa's root guru. Still, in the final sense, our root guru is the one through whose instruction and pointing out we recognize our buddha nature.

c. As far as the lama of blessing is concerned, there is no limitation whatsoever. This type of lama is any person from whom we have learned something that helped us to improve ourselves toward enlightenment.

d. A lama in the general sense is anybody who upholds the lineage of Lord Buddha's teaching and does so purely, no matter whether we have learned something from him or whether he belongs to the same school as ourselves.

The essence of all these different types of lamas is the pure teaching of Lord Buddha (Tib. *dé sheg ka'i la ma*). Here, *dé sheg* means "buddha," and *ka* means "command," "word," or "teaching." This is the real lama: the teaching of the Buddha. Any human being who upholds this teaching, who cherishes, preserves, and propagates it, is a lama. Without the teaching of the Buddha, the lama, by definition, does not exist.

When the Karmapa refers to lamas in the plural (*la ma nam*), he refers to all the lamas mentioned above, not excluding a single one.

2. Next he addresses the yidams and the deities of the mandala. Technically speaking this is a repetition since there is no yidam apart from the deities of the mandala, but in this context "yidam" refers to the main deity at the center of the mandala, and "deities of the mandala" refers to the retinue of this deity. Some mandalas are formed by

up to a thousand deities, while some consist of only one, or five, and so forth.

What is to be understood by "yidam" or "deity" has already been explained above to a certain extent. The central deity is the sambhogakaya aspect of the Buddha himself. In this aspect, he taught a particular tantra, this tantra being equivalent to his manifestation and represented in the form of the deity, while his environment manifested as the surrounding of this deity, thus forming a mandala. The meaning of the mandala is this particular tantra.

In this way, each tantra has its own mandala; the deity and its environment represent the higher, tantric aspect of Lord Buddha's manifestation and the teachings that are part of it.

3. The Karmapa then addresses the "victorious ones of the ten directions and three times, together with their sons." "Victorious One" or "Glorious One" is an epithet of the Buddha. This term is used because by overcoming and conquering the ego, our basic ignorance which consists of attachment to a self and of everything that accompanies it, we become liberated and enlightened. Enlightenment is ultimate victory and glory.

The sons of the buddha are the bodhisattvas, though of course bodhisattvas can be male like Avalokiteshvara and Manjushri or female like Tara. The term refers to the example of the son of a king: if the prince performs well and does not fail, he will succeed his father and become king himself. In light of this example, the scriptures always speak of "sons of the Buddha" rather than of "daughters of the Buddha." Though I am not a feminist, I think this is due to a certain chauvinism that existed at the time in those countries where the scriptures were composed: only the son of a king could become king himself, while the king's daughter could not succeed her father but could only become a queen through being married to another king. If there were no female bodhisattvas, one might say there must be some fixed reason for calling a bodhisattva a son of the Buddha, but since there are so many female bodhisattvas the reason must be purely cultural. I personally do not believe in either male chauvinism or feminism; they are the same to me. In my view both these attitudes are totally samsaric. This does not mean that we should not do something when somebody is going too far: it is perfectly all right to put such a person in his or her place. But men and women are equally part of samsara; neither is better than the other. We had therefore best just be human!

When the Karmapa speaks of the buddhas and bodhisattvas "of the ten directions and three times" this has a very deep meaning, as through this phrase we can understand exactly what a buddha or a bodhisattva is. Otherwise we might view the Buddha as some extraordinary entity who appeared two thousand five hundred years ago and that was it. We could merely consider

ourselves his followers but have nothing to do with him.
The Buddha could be just some kind of eye-opener up
there. Instead, there are the buddhas of the ten directions
and the three times, which is to say, there is not just one
buddha: in the past there have always been buddhas, there
are buddhas now, and there will be buddhas forever in
the future. The presence of bodhisattvas is to be understood in the same way: there are bodhisattvas in the ten
directions and the three times. This expresses clearly what
a bodhisattva is. A bodhisattva does not necessarily have
to be a Buddhist. Every sentient being is buddha; this is
much more than just being a Buddhist. We are very fortunate that the Buddha attained enlightenment not too
long ago, and that his teaching and lineage are still alive;
we do not have to invent our own teachings, but are able
to learn and practice the living teaching of Lord Buddha.
We take advantage of this fact and enjoy the privilege it
offers. Yet this does not mean that the present Buddhist
way is the only one to reach enlightenment. Present Buddhism started after Lord Buddha's enlightenment; it did
not exist before. The Buddha managed to attain enlightenment without the present form of Buddhism; therefore
every sentient being in the ten directions and the three
times will manage to do the same. I do not think that our
present Buddhist publications reach that far! They do not
even cover our planet earth sufficiently, so there is no need
to think of other places! In this way, the phrase "buddhas

and bodhisattvas of the ten directions and three times" conveys a clear notion of the meaning of being a Buddhist, the meaning of being a bodhisattva, and the meaning of enlightenment, or buddhahood.

As for some further explanation of the term "bodhisattva," its definition is very specific. Sometimes "bodhisattva" is misunderstood as simply meaning somebody who has concern for other sentient beings, and who cares for them. Although this is very good, and constitutes one of a bodhisattva's ways of dealing with others, it does not make a person a bodhisattva. The defining characteristic of a bodhisattva is the development of bodhichitta, the wish to attain enlightenment in order to benefit beings; once this wish has arisen one becomes a bodhisattva. When we like to give people food, clothing, and shelter, this is very good; a bodhisattva should do these things if it is the best he or she can do, but through such actions alone we will not become bodhisattvas. A bodhisattva is someone who is inspired by the aspiration to realize enlightenment for the benefit of all sentient beings. This is bodhichitta, the characteristic of a bodhisattva. To understand this definition is quite important, as it describes somebody who is wise as opposed to someone who is a very good person but not necessarily enlightened. Thus, the definition of who is a bodhisattva is directly related to enlightenment, to buddhahood.

The Tibetan expression for bodhichitta is *jang chub kyi sem*. Here, *jang chub* means "enlightenment," and *sem* means "mind"; *kyi* is a particle indicating that "enlightenment" describes a type of "mind." Thus the phrase means "mind of enlightenment," or "mind focused on enlightenment." The word for bodhisattva, *jang chub sem pa*, means one who has this *jang chub kyi sem*. The word for buddhahood also uses these terms: it is called *jang chub kyi go pang*, or "the state of enlightenment." So all these are interrelated; in this way the term "bodhisattva" is totally connected with enlightenment.

Still, it is impossible to develop bodhichitta, the aspiration to attain enlightenment for the sake of all sentient beings, without caring for these beings. If someone is a bodhisattva, invariably kindness will be there. But it will not be limited to smiling—it will be a kindness that makes use of all the necessary means, not just of the easy ones. Bodhichitta is easy to talk about, but in practice it is not that easy; in practice it can be quite tricky, and one can easily be misled. Bodhisattvas can make mistakes in their practice, but they mend them immediately, without holding on to them. A bodhisattva might be stubborn, but not stubborn enough to justify his or her mistakes!

4. The Karmapa then prays: "Please consider me with kindness and grant your blessing." This is a paradox. The Buddha has no limitation, so to ask him: "consider me and grant your blessing" is paradoxical. Nevertheless, this

is how it works. As long as we call ourselves "I" and perceive ourselves in a dualistic way, we definitely have to start with the "I." If, for instance, one tries to overcome a person's ego, there has to be an ego first; if the ego is very slippery and blurred, there is hardly any basis since there is no structured ego to work upon. It is very difficult to help somebody overcome his or her problems when the problems are unstructured, when in a certain way this person does not have any problems, though deep inside all the problems are there. It is very difficult for a human being whose problem is confused, whose ego is ill-defined and without foundation, to really purify, clarify, and develop anything.

The same principle applies to praying. As long as we have our self, our ego, we pray to the Buddha: "Please bless me so that my prayers for the benefit of all sentient beings be fulfilled." Otherwise our prayer does not follow any line or direction. It would be like going to a big five-star hotel with five hundred rooms and not knowing your room number, or taking an elevator without knowing which floor to go to—this would be a big problem. This is the reason for calling upon the great compassion of the Buddha and asking him to consider our prayers. The reason is not that the Buddha only listens to someone who prays to him; rather, without praying to the Buddha we are not developed enough to have the condition necessary to receive his blessing. Rain might be falling for ten thousand years, yet if our cup is upside down it will remain empty. Through praying we open up, we turn our cup to let the water get inside. This is why the Karmapa has written these lines. I do not mean to say that the Karmapa has an ego. He has written this for us to pray. I definitely have an ego and I guess you have too.

In the last line the Karmapa says: "May it become conducive to my supplications being fulfilled as they are." The term "conducive" (Tib. *tün gyur*) denotes a positive condition, a facilitation. This has a very deep meaning, indicating that the blessing of the Buddha, or any kind of blessing, is just a facilitation. The Buddha's blessing cannot force us to become enlightened. If this were the case, why are we not already enlightened? Why did the Buddha leave us here for two thousand five hundred years? Why did he not make all sentient beings enlightened right after he had attained enlightenment himself? The blessing of the Buddha does not function this way, since we are equal to him in our ultimate potential. The Buddha cannot impose anything upon us because his ultimate reality and our ultimate reality are the same. We are not less than the Buddha, yet the definition of enlightenment consists of the fact that we have to realize that we are buddha. This realization will not come about by walking out and shouting: "I am buddha!" This would just lead us to be taken to a nice little retreat for a few days! We have to recognize that our ultimate potential is buddha, and we have to become buddha in terms of an inner realization; this does not come from somewhere else, as if somebody injected buddha into our brain. For this reason, every blessing that we request constitutes a facilitation, a favorable condition for our prayers to come true. The blessing makes everything easier, more positive and conducive. This is the meaning of *tün gyur.* It has nothing to do with imposing or forcing anything, or playing tricks by which we are manipulated into enlightenment. Enlightenment has to happen for real.

5. In the four lines that constitute the preliminary part of the prayer, the Third Karmapa makes it very clear whom he is addressing and out of what motivation he does so. His motivation consists of the wish that everything he states in what follows may be fulfilled. This means that the Karmapa considers whatever he says in this prayer to be of great importance to himself, to his disciples, and to all sentient beings. At the same time, this being a Mahamudra prayer, its entire content is in accordance with the Mahamudra teaching and principle, and it expresses all important points in light of the Mahamudra understanding.

When the Karmapa prays to the lamas, yidams, deities of the mandala, buddhas, and bodhisattvas, he prays to the three jewels and the three roots simultaneously. While the buddhas and bodhisattvas are mentioned explicitly, the Dharma is not; the Dharma is contained in his addressing the lamas. The *dé sheg ka'i la ma*, the lama in terms of the words of the Buddha, is the Dharma, the most important aspect of Dharma. The protectors are also not mentioned explicitly. They are included in his praying to the bodhisattvas and to the deities of the mandala; the protectors have specific mandalas and are part of many yidam deities' mandalas. Finally, the fact that, of the three roots, the lama is addressed first shows that this is a Vajrayana prayer, Mahamudra being the highest aspect of Vajrayana teaching. In this way the Karmapa clearly points out to which system this prayer belongs, to whom he prays, and for what aim.

## Part Two: The Supplications

This section contains the actual supplications, which are divided into two main parts: firstly a general supplication for the attainment of great liberation, and secondly specific supplications.

> **May the streams of the accumulation of virtue**
> **rise from the snow-mountain**
> **Of the pure intention and action of myself and**
> **all beings limitless in number.**
> **May these streams be free from the cloudiness**
> **of the three wheels**
> **And thus flow into the ocean of the four kayas**
> **of the Victorious One.**

In brief the meaning of this supplication is as follows: May the pure motivation and pure action of myself and of all beings, infinite in number, be free from any kind of dualistic notion. May we attain the great liberation, enlightenment.

To compose these four lines the Karmapa used a particular type of poetry known as "combination" (Tib. *jar wa*). This type of poetry makes use of metaphors—the subject is not likened to an example but is figuratively expressed by means of it. Here the image of water is used three times, and all three images are connected with each other. Water is first seen as snow on the mountain; the snow then melts and goes into the river; finally, the river slowly runs to the sea. Throughout, the water is the same, though it undergoes a continuous process of change. This sequence is used to express the process of enlightenment.

When the Karmapa speaks of "myself and all beings limitless in number," he indicates explicitly that sentient beings are beyond count. This corresponds to basic Buddhist philosophy, particularly to that part of Lord Buddha's teaching called Abhidharma, in which the Buddha describes very clearly that space has no end, that universes have no end, and that the number of sentient beings is infinite. In this way there are countless sentient beings filling countless universes within endless space.

As a general supplication for the attainment of enlightenment, this verse represents the entire text of the Mahamudra prayer except for the conclusion. If one summarizes the content of the second part, it is contained in these four lines expressing the wish that ourselves and all sentient beings may accumulate merit, and that this merit, all the good things we do and think, may become pure enough to be a useful condition for reaching enlightenment. Then we dedicate this merit toward that aim. This is the purpose and content of the whole text.

The fourth line describes the goal. Here the Karmapa wishes: May all our good deeds result in the great liberation of the Victorious One. Literally he speaks of "the ocean of the four kayas," which is another way of describing enlightenment, the state of a buddha. The third line points out what types of good deeds will be positive conditions for reaching great liberation. This is shown through the image of a pure stream, free from the cloudiness of the three wheels or spheres. The three spheres are agent, object, and their interaction. Freedom from these can be understood by means of the following example. If one gives something to somebody, this is a dualistic action, in that there is a giver, there is somebody to give to, and there is something to be given. When we try to turn our activity of giving into a means of reaching enlightenment, it should be as selfless a gift as possible: we should not expect any appreciation, any kind of reward or glory, honor or anything else; we should just give. Then we may wonder how long we should continue giving, and the answer is: until we have overcome the total dualism of giving. This is the only purpose. If the aim were to continue giving until the whole world overflowed with abundance, this would be impossible. It is the self, dualism, that we have to overcome. This constitutes the type of profound virtue that we should accumulate. The same principle applies to everything else—to any prayer, meditation, or form of discipline, to being moral, diligent, tolerant, and so forth. This is the content of the third line.

From the preceding lines we can see very clearly the means to free positive action, virtuous action, from dualism: these are pure motivation and action. Through these means our deeds become selfless, since pure motivation is selfless motivation—if our purpose in doing something good is the purpose pursued by a bodhisattva, we act for the sake of enlightenment, for the benefit of all sentient beings, and in this way our actions become naturally less dualistic. If we do somebody good because we deem ourselves better than that person, or because we see somebody in trouble and just want to help that person out of trouble, although there is nothing wrong with such action, it is not non-dualistic. The means to achieve non-dualistic action are called *sam jor nam dag* in Tibetan. *Sam pa* means "motivation," or "thought," or "intention," while *jor wa* is the actual application of this motivation—the deed itself. *Nam dag* means "utterly pure." The example for this pure intention and action is a snow-mountain, the snows of which melt and become a river; thus the snow-mountain is the source of the river.

To summarize the verse: the Karmapa supplicates that all the positive things that he and all sentient beings accomplish through good motivation and action may be free from the threefold dualistic bondage, and thus result in enlightenment. He prays that all these good deeds may become the causes and conditions for great liberation. This sets out the basic purpose of his supplication, as well as the reason for the particular prayers that follow. They contain important details necessary for a practitioner's actions to become positive conditions for liberation, instead of becoming positive conditions for samsara, or even for a limited release that does not constitute total liberation.

Everything in this world that has something good about it, every pleasure, happiness, joy, and comfort, results from having done something good. It is not the result of bad action. If positive activity becomes the cause of this kind of well-being, this is good, but for someone who tries to practice the Vajrayana it could be close to disaster! Though this is slightly exaggerated, it could be ruinous in that joy and comfort can corrupt us much more than suffering. The purpose for which the Third Karmapa has written this prayer is, therefore, to ensure that our good deeds do not become another condition that will bury us more deeply in the cycle of existence. If it were possible to become enlightened very comfortably, with a lot of convenience and little effort, we should definitely wish for that. But the Karmapa makes it very clear that the mere doing of something good is no guarantee for achieving a good result. For instance, a person who does not have any power can be very bad but is not able to do very much apart from shouting, while if someone wields great power and is negative, he or she can do a lot of damage. The same is true for good things, of course. The Karmapa is indicating the means that will protect us from our good deeds having negative results. It is vital to understand that good deeds are good, yet, if they are not complete according to the principles taught by the Buddha in the context of the Mahayana, they do not guarantee a result that is exclusively good.

A few particular topics should be explained in slightly more detail. As far as motivation and action (Tib. *sam pa* and *jor wa*) are concerned, motivation always refers to the mind, while action refers to body and speech. Thus the three aspects of body, speech, and mind divide into two. Action comes about through body and speech; intention stems from the mind.

When the Karmapa mentions the four kayas of the Victorious One he refers to dharmakaya, sambhogakaya, nirmanakaya, and svabhavikakaya. Of these the svabhavikakaya (Tib. *ngo wo nyi kyi ku*) is not a further form of manifestation, but denotes the fact that the dharmakaya, sambhogakaya, and nirmanakaya are not separate from each other. They are just three different aspects of the state of a buddha, which is indivisible.

A last thing that should be clarified in the context of explaining this prayer is the fact that enlightenment is impossible without bodhichitta. A bodhisattva need not necessarily be a follower of Buddhism, but bodhichitta, the mind focused on enlightenment, must be present. This means that enlightenment does not happen by surprise, nor by mistake or accident.

## II. SPECIFIC SUPPLICATIONS

These divide into five parts. The first refers to the completeness of the conditions necessary to follow the path, in this context the practice of Mahamudra leading to liberation. The second refers to the wisdom necessary to comprehend the depth of this path, while the third describes the correct unmistaken path itself. The fourth contains prayers toward gaining the ability to pursue this unmistaken path correctly, and the fifth refers to the aspect of fruition, the result achieved through completing the pursuit of the path.

### A. THE CONDITIONS NECESSARY TO FOLLOW THE PATH

There are two kinds, the ordinary and the special conditions.

### 1. THE ORDINARY NECESSARY CONDITION

> **As long as this is not attained, in all our future
>    lifetimes,
> Birth upon birth, may not even the sound
> Of evildoing and suffering be heard.
> May we enjoy the glory of an ocean of virtue
>    and happiness**

When the Karmapa says: "as long as this is not attained," "this" refers to the foregoing verse, to the ocean of the four kayas of the Victorious One. He expresses the wish that throughout all the time it will take us to attain enlightenment, life upon life, we may not commit any negative deeds, and thus may be free from suffering. Without negative action there is no suffering, not even the sound of it.

One may wonder why this is a necessary condition. If we commit negative actions, or if we are forced to engage in negative activity, this becomes an adverse condition that will prevent us from reaching enlightenment. For this reason we pray that we will not have to commit any negative deeds, that there will not be even the tendency to do so. If, for instance, we were born in hell or as an amoeba, an earthworm, a frog, or something similar, spiritual development would be very difficult, though not totally impossible. Bodhisattvas can be born in such existences, as is shown by the Buddha, who was born as a monkey, a rabbit, and so forth. Yet if we just become an ordinary frog, it is very difficult to survive. This kind of existence contains so much constant fear and anxiety, and many various sufferings, most of which we cannot even imagine since we are no longer subject to them. The results having faded, we are liberated from many things that we once did, and which would constitute a great hindrance to our development and maturation. Therefore we pray not to have to commit any more negative actions. This may not sound utterly profound—this is why the Karmapa calls it the ordinary condition—but it is the starting point we have to achieve first. If, for instance, we had to live in circumstances that forced us to earn our living by actions much more negative than humans have to carry out, enlightenment would be quite difficult; likewise, if there were no conditions whatsoever to allow us to do positive things, or if there were no common moral principles at all, we would find it very hard to even figure out what is good and what is bad.

While this verse sets out the basic, fundamental condition, it implicitly indicates that there are other possibilities— we might find ourselves in a totally different environment, in a different historical situation and subject to completely different conditions. Nowadays the term *kali yuga* is used frequently. Our present eon is often referred to as a *kali yuga,* or time of degeneration, but in fact there is much that is positive about our world. For example, if someone beats another person up, nobody will like this; there is a common understanding that this is a negative action. Or if somebody steals from someone, it is a general moral principle to condemn this behavior; a person will even be put into prison for stealing. In this way our world contains a great deal of real light.

A *kali yuga,* though, is completely different. *Yuga* is a Sanskrit term meaning "eon." The time span between the beginning and the end of a universe is called a "greater *yuga,*" and consists of countless centuries. A greater *yuga* (Tib. *kalpa*) is divided into different periods called "intermediate *yuga.*" These refer to ups and downs, for example as human society passes through different stages.

The defining characteristic of a *kali yuga* is the fact that from the beginning of a particular universe until its end, no one attains enlightenment. This can easily come to pass. Under these conditions such a universe will be bereft of anything that is positive. Everybody kills everybody else, and just eats anything, like animals in the mountains. There are no moral principles, no support for right and wrong or for anything good, just a constant process of killing and devouring each other. This is the definition of the term *kali yuga:* the term *kali* means "darkness."

As opposed to this, the Karmapa prays that we may be reborn in a *saté yuga* (*saté* means "light"), with good, positive circumstances as the general condition. In the following verses he describes the specific conditions necessary for the practice of the Vajrayana.

The terms *kali yuga* and *saté yuga* are sometimes misinterpreted. There are certain universes that are far away from any source of light and therefore always in total darkness; the sentient beings there do not have eyes. Such universes are also described by the Buddha as "dark universes," whereas our universe is bright, in that it has light, day and night, suns and stars. It is a mistake, though, to call these universes *kali yuga* and *saté yuga,* and if one were to carefully examine the scriptures, this mistake would not occur.

In the same way, our time is one of degeneration, but it is not a *kali yuga.* In this present eon a thousand buddhas will attain enlightenment; Buddha Shakyamuni is the fourth of these, so there are more than nine hundred and ninety buddhas still to come. Therefore the Buddha describes our eon as a fortunate one. In the *Fortunate Eon Sutra* (Tib. *Do dé kalpa sangpo*), the Buddha prophesied the names of a thousand buddhas; the next to appear will be Buddha Maitreya, who is predicted to attain enlightenment as the fifth of these buddhas about two million years from now.

The basic condition necessary to be able to practice the Dharma is therefore to be born in a fortunate eon, and this is what we have achieved at present. Within the time span between Buddha Shakyamuni and Buddha Maitreya countless sentient beings who have not been prophesied, like Guru Rinpoche, Milarepa, and so forth, will attain enlightenment. I am quite sure that some of those present here will be enlightened before Lord Maitreya reaches enlightenment. Even some of the sentient beings living in our bodies as bacteria may get enlightened in the meantime. In this way so much that is wonderful will happen in our eon that we can never seriously call it a *kali yuga.* Some traditions do so but this is only a popular expression, a conventional way of speaking, just as we say: "This is human nature..." when someone does something that is not quite nice. This saying is justified to a certain extent, since most human beings are used to doing negative things. In truth, though, human nature is not bad; it is buddha.

*2. THE SPECIAL NECESSARY CONDITION*

> **Having attained supreme leisure and endowment, possessing faith, diligence, and wisdom,**
> **Having relied on a good spiritual friend and received the essence of his instructions,**
> **May we practice them properly without any hindrance,**
> **And thus enact the sacred Dharma in all our future lives.**

In order to be able to follow the path of the Vajrayana, first we must have obtained a precious human life. Then we have to develop devotion, diligence, and wisdom; we need to find a good teacher and receive his or her profound instructions; in practicing these we should be as free from any obstacles as possible; and we pray that such practice may continue life after life. The meeting of all these factors constitutes the special good condition necessary to practice Mahamudra.

*B. THE WISDOM NECESSARY TO COMPREHEND THE DEPTH OF THE PATH*

> **Through studying the words of the Buddha and the treatises of logic, we are freed from the veil of unknowing.**

> Through reflecting upon the oral instructions,
> we overcome the darkness of doubt.
> Through the light born from meditation, the
> true nature shines forth as it is.
> May the brilliance of the three wisdoms spread.

The meaning of this supplication is as follows. Through hearing the teachings of the Buddha, as well as studying the treatises on logic and the commentaries interpreting the words of the Buddha, our ignorance will be eliminated. Through contemplating the instructions we receive we will clarify our doubts. Through meditation we will gain clear realization of reality as it is. These are considered as three types of wisdom, the wisdoms resulting from studying, reflection, and meditation. We therefore pray for the development of these.

*C. THE CORRECT UNMISTAKEN PATH*

> The two truths which are free from the extremes
> of eternalism and nihilism are the meaning
> of the ground.
> Through the supreme path of the two accumula-
> tions, which is free from the extremes of
> assertion and denial,
> We attain the fruit, the twofold benefit, which
> is free from the extremes of existence and
> mere peace.
> May we meet this Dharma, unmistaken and
> free from error.

This prayer means that ground-Mahamudra should consist of a clear view that is neither eternalistic nor nihilistic. The path we follow should be free from denial and assertion, and the fruition to be finally reached should be free from both extremes of samsara and a limited nirvana in the sense of mere peace. In this way our path will not lead us in a wrong direction, and not in a mistaken direction, either. We therefore pray that we may follow this unmistaken path. (For further explanation of the terms used in this verse, see Appendix.)

*D. THE PRACTICE OF THE PATH*

The supplications concerning the practice of the path have two parts, the first being a general prayer and the second containing specific details.

*1. GENERAL SUPPLICATION TOWARD THE PRACTICE OF THE PATH*

> **The ground to be purified is the mind itself,**
> **the union of clarity and emptiness.**
> **The means of purification is the great vajra-yoga**
> **of Mahamudra.**
> **What is to be removed are the adventitious**
> **stains of delusion.**
> **The fruit of purification is the dharmakaya free**
> **from stains. Through these means may it**
> **reveal itself directly.**

Through this prayer, the entire practice of the path is introduced in terms of a process of purification. In this context the ground, or the basis to be purified, is the mind which is empty and at the same time clear, the union of emptiness and clarity. The method to achieve this purification is

Mahamudra meditation, which is called "vajra yoga," since by this practice the ordinary body, speech, and mind are transformed into a special, extraordinary body, speech, and mind. Everything that is negative is transformed into the positive. That which is to be removed are karma, the defilements, and so forth, which are adventitious, temporary obstacles able to be removed. The fruit of this process of purification is the unstained dharmakaya which is the essence of every sentient being; fruition is achieved when this essence is realized. We therefore pray to attain this realization.

### 2. SPECIFIC SUPPLICATIONS TOWARD THE PRACTICE OF THE PATH

These are particular prayers for the actual application of the means of purification. They also consist of two parts: a general prayer, and the details.

### a. GENERAL SUPPLICATION

> **Cutting our doubts with regard to the ground
>     brings conviction of the view.
> Preserving this without distraction is the
>     essence of meditation.
> Skillfully enacting the meaning of meditation
>     in everything is supreme conduct.
> May we gain certainty in the view, meditation,
>     and conduct.**

This prayer describes view, meditation, and action. The view consists of determining the basis, which is ground-Mahamudra. To preserve this ground that we have determined, which is to say to observe the nature of our mind, is meditation. Once we master meditation we are able to maintain the recognition and realization of the nature of our mind, and this continuation is our action. Action is to be understood in the sense that, whether or not one meditates, one will remain in the state of Mahamudra— awareness and clear realization of the nature of the mind. Thus our action is also practice: our action is blessed by the meditation, transformed by the meditation. This view, this meditation, and this action are what need to be developed. So we pray for this development.

*b. DETAILED SUPPLICATIONS*

These consist of three groups of prayers, the first describing the view; the second, the meditation; and the third, the action.

*b.1. SUPPLICATIONS PERTAINING TO THE VIEW*

These also fall into two parts, a concise supplication and detailed supplications.

*b.1.a. CONCISE SUPPLICATION PERTAINING TO THE VIEW*

> **All phenomena are illusory manifestations of
> our mind.
> As for the mind, there is no mind: it is empty
> of essence.
> It is empty and yet unceasingly appears
> everywhere.
> Investigating well, may we discern the
> fundamental root.**

This prayer contains the wish that everything may be realized as being the manifestation of mind. Our mind does not exist as something solid; it does not have any dualistic reality. Although it is devoid of dualistic reality and thus beyond this limitation, at the same time it manifests as everything. We therefore pray that by profoundly observing our mind in its true being we may determine our ground, our basic potential, which is the working basis for enlightenment.

### b.1.b. DETAILED SUPPLICATIONS PERTAINING TO THE VIEW

The detailed supplications consist of five particular prayers. The first refers to the fact that everything we see and perceive is a manifestation or the vision of our mind. The second prayer points out that mind should not be viewed as being existent, nor as being non-existent either; it is beyond any limitation in terms of having a solid reality or of being nothing at all. The third shows our mind as not being something that can be compared to anything; it cannot be described in such terms as "it is like this" or "it is not like this." The fourth prayer teaches the union of emptiness and interdependence. The fifth contains the wish to gain final certainty as to the basic ground. In this context the term "ground" (Tib. *shi*) refers to the limitless potential that is present within all sentient beings; one can also use the term "foundation," though this is not to be misunderstood in terms of those types of practice called "the foundations." If, for instance, one is searching for subterranean oil reserves, one first needs a ground, in that one has to find out whether there is oil or not; otherwise there would be no point in trying to produce it—one might labor and not find anything. Likewise, if sentient beings did not have buddha nature and yet tried to practice the Dharma and tried to be good, this would be absolutely futile; there would not be any ground, it would be just imagination. But sentient beings have buddha nature—this is the working basis for any type of Buddhist practice. When in the context of Mahamudra the terms "ground," "path," and "fruition" are used, this is what is meant by the term "ground."

*b.1.b.1. EVERYTHING IS THE MANIFESTATION OF THE MIND*

> **Self-appearance which never existed is mistaken**
> **for an object.**
> **Under the domination of ignorance, self-aware-**
> **ness is mistaken for a self.**
> **By the power of dualistic fixation we wander**
> **through the realm of existence.**
> **May we eradicate our ignorant delusion.**

Based upon statements in this prayer, some scholars hold the Mahamudra view to be less valid than that of the Madhyamaka. Seeing that in the context of the Mahamudra everything is said to be a manifestation of the mind, they claim that the view of the Mahamudra corresponds to that of the Chittamatra or "Mind Only" school. All our great masters disagree with this opinion and I totally disagree with it as well. Its coming about is comparable to the traditional Tibetan saying: "If you think too much, your head will spin like an umbrella!" Since nowadays people do not spin umbrellas any more, one should maybe use the example of a yo-yo. It is the outcome of a shallow and extreme thought that these scholars try to impose on others.

The correct view becomes very clear in the four lines of this prayer. Mahamudra is the essence of Chittamatra as well as of Madhyamaka; Mahamudra is the essence of everything. According to this view all aspects of external reality do not have any existence beyond their being the object of mind. But in contradiction to this they are mistakenly perceived as true realities existing out there. This can be illustrated by the following example. Someone who has hepatitis perceives everything as having a yellow tinge. This does not mean, though, that all the visible objects that he or she sees are yellow: the perception of the yellow color comes from inside. When we look at ourselves, at our mind, we mistakenly perceive it in terms of an "I." Once we are able to overcome this misconception we will always see our buddha nature. Yet, as long as this is mistaken for an "I," for just one thing, a limited entity, that which is greatest becomes what is smallest and most miserable. Mind is like space, but once we call it "I" we turn it into the smallest and most limited thing. This is the definition of samsara, since as long as we are subject to this dualism between an existing self and outwardly existing entities, we are in samsara. The perception of this dualism is ignorance. We therefore pray that we may eliminate our unknowing.

*b.1.b.2. MIND IS NEITHER EXISTENT NOR NON-EXISTENT*

**It is not existent, since even the Victorious One does not see it.**
**It is not non-existent, since it is the basis of everything, of samsara and nirvana.**
**These not being contradictory, it is unity, the path of the middle.**
**May we realize the true state of our mind, which is free from any extreme.**

The meaning of this prayer is as follows. When we meditate on our mind we should not view it as a solid and truly existing entity. The reason given is that the Buddha does not see it this way. This is to say that the realization of the Buddha did not come about through seeing the mind in terms of solid reality, but by realizing that the essence of mind is limitless; it is therefore not a visible object that can be seen in the conventional way. It does not mean that there is something to be seen which the Buddha was not able to see, but that gaining certainty that mind does not exist as a solid entity is part of the realization of the Buddha. On the other hand it cannot be nothing, since the entirety of samsara and nirvana is based upon it. It comprises all those sentient beings who incessantly cling to their "I" as well as all the buddhas and bodhisattvas who manifest as the embodiment of compassion in order to liberate these sentient beings. In this way it is the basis of everything.

So mind is neither something solid nor is it nothing at all. These two aspects are not contradictory, for which fact we ourselves provide evidence. We are here. Our mind does not constitute a solid reality, yet at the same time we can think and are able to understand. Some of us have a better realization of this union, some a lesser; some do not believe in it at all, some see and understand it clearly. In this way it is reality and not a conflict. Truly seeing the non-dualistic nature of the mind, which is union, which has no solid reality and yet is the essence of everything, we follow the Middle Way. This is part of the Madhyamaka system. In this context we pray that we may realize the nature of our mind as being limitless, beyond any extreme.

*b.1.b.3. MIND IS INDESCRIBABLE*

> **There is no way to illustrate it, saying "it is this."**
> **There is no way to refute it, saying "it is not this."**
> **The true state is beyond intellect, it is uncreated.**
> **May the ultimate true meaning be confirmed.**

This verse refers to the fact that mind cannot be described by means of any example except mind itself. One cannot pinpoint it, saying "It is like this." Since this is not possible, one cannot illustrate it either by the opposite, by saying "It is not like this." Mind is just mind and the nature of our mind has to be experienced through realization; it cannot be experienced in any other way, through any kind of analogy or example. Mind is inconceivable, it is beyond thoughts and concepts; thoughts result from not having realized the nature of mind, and for this reason the description will never be accurate as long as thoughts are used to discover or describe the nature of mind. With these means one can illustrate it to a certain small extent, but its final recognition has to take place through realization. And mind is not composite. It is not the result of various factors having come together; it does not consist of atoms, molecules, and so forth. All of this is part of relative truth, whereas the mind is ultimate truth. In light of this understanding we pray that we may gain the ability to realize the nature of our mind, which is the final ultimate truth.

*b.1.b.4. THE UNION OF EMPTINESS AND INTERDEPENDENCE*

> **As long as this is not realized, we circle in the ocean of samsara.**
> **Once it is realized, buddha is nowhere else.**
> **Every [notion of] "it is this" or "it is not this" has fallen away.**
> **May we be aware of the true state, the hidden secret of our basis-consciousness.**

The union of emptiness and interdependence is to be understood as follows. As long as we have not realized the nature of our mind we are subject to the normal course of the twelve links of interdependent origination. Absence of realization is ignorance and from this starting point the subsequent eleven links will form one after the other, each giving rise to the next. Thus everything continues in one way. However, once we realize the nature of our mind, the links of interdependent origination are traced back to their source and in this way dissolved: when there is no ignorance the other links cannot come about. This is emptiness. Once emptiness is realized, this is enlightenment. Emptiness is limitless and therefore beyond any definition in terms of "It is this," "It is not this," and so forth; it cannot be restricted to such limitations. When the nature of mind is realized, this proves to be the nature of all phenomena (Tib. *chö nyi*, Skt. *dharmata*), the essence of everything. This is what is meant here by the term "basis-consciousness" (Skt. *alaya*). The secret of the essence of everything is the fact that everything is buddha and thus beyond any limitation. In my view this is quite easy to understand once the proper connection is made. Without this it could be quite complicated. The fact, for instance, that the term "alaya" is used might lead to the notion that the Mahamudra view is identical to that of the Chittamatra system, as I have mentioned already. The forming of such an opinion, though, can be compared to the following example. Suppose some blind people were to investigate what an elephant looks like. One of them might touch a leg and thereupon claim that an elephant looks like a tree; another might feel the stomach and come to the conclusion that an elephant is similar to a big pot, and a third upon touching its tail might say that an elephant is like a rope. Yet, as soon as there is somebody kind enough to point out that the legs of an elephant look like trees while its stomach is similar to a big pot and its tail to a rope, the matter becomes very easy. This is where the lineage comes into play. Someone who is part of the lineage will never say an elephant looks like a tree, since this person has seen the elephant.

### b.1.b.5. FINAL CERTAINTY AS TO THE BASIC GROUND

**Appearance is mind and emptiness is mind.**
**Realization is mind and delusion is mind.**
**Arising is mind and cessation is also mind.**
**Therefore, cutting all doubts, may we confirm**
**everything as mind.**

I think the words of this prayer are quite easy to understand and do not need any further explanation. They clarify that, once the nature of mind is realized, everything will be determined.

### b.2. SUPPLICATIONS PERTAINING TO THE MEDITATION

These also fall into two parts, one concise prayer and six detailed ones.

*b.2.a. CONCISE SUPPLICATION PERTAINING TO THE MEDITATION*

**Not adulterated by a meditation bound up with
conceptual strife,
And unmoved by the wind of ordinary bustle,
May we know how to abide naturally at ease
in our uncontrived innermost nature.
May we become skilled in this practice of the
meaning of mind, and maintain it.**

This means that as far as meditation or practice is concerned, we should not be involved with its dualistic aspect. This should be as minimal as possible. And definitely we should be aware and make sure not to be shaken by the ordinary activity of body, speech, and mind; this is especially true regarding any ordinary mental activity. When we manage to remain in a state that is unchanged, pure, and original, we are able to meditate on quite a profound level of Mahamudra. Thus Mahamudra meditation is described as meditation on the nature of mind. We therefore pray: May I have the ability to meditate on the nature of my mind and to maintain this meditation. This constitutes a very particular aspect of Mahamudra meditation.

As a practitioner, though, and especially as a beginner, one has to make use of dualism. One has to think: "Now I am meditating; my teacher told me how to do this; next I do this," and so forth. These kinds of thoughts are inevitable, but we should try as best as we can to keep other

thoughts to a minimum. To ensure this, it is most important for a practitioner who is a beginner not to introduce
his or her own ideas on meditation into the practice; we
should just meditate and use whatever practice we have
received through the lineage. This is the first step, to avoid
and minimize any dualistic involvement. When in consequence we are really able to perceive the clarity of the
nature of our mind we should try to remain within non-
duality, to be as non-dualistic as possible. Though if we
feel compelled to think: "I have to be non-dualistic!" this
is a duality far greater than the one that is already there!
So we should just sit and remain in our innate original
being (Tib. *ma chö nyug ma*). Here, *ma chö* means "unchanged," "uncorrected," or "unaltered": there is nothing to be added and nothing to be removed. It also means
"original." We should therefore just sit and abide within
our ultimate nature, the original state of our mind, without being involved in any mental activity or dualism. This
is what we attempt to achieve, and when we have gained
this ability we will have become quite highly enlightened
Mahamudra practitioners. On the path toward this goal
we try to minimize our physical, oral, and mental activity during meditation practice. The stage of meditation
described in this verse is not far from the stage of
buddhahood. When really mastered it almost equals the
first realization of Mahamudra.

There are six specific supplications pertaining to the meditation that is described above. The first prayer refers to calm abiding (Tib. *shi né*), and the second to special or vivid insight (Tib. *lhag tong*). The third describes the way of seeing in the state of special insight during the post-meditative phase. The fourth prayer illustrates the simultaneous presence (Tib. *sung jug*) or union of calm abiding and special insight. The fifth refers to what is called "experience" (Tib. *nyam*), in that it represents a sense of accomplishment or achievement. It can be said to be a glimpse of realization. The sixth describes the actual achievement or realization itself (Tib. *tog pa*). It is quite exciting to have the type of meditation experience called *nyam*, while the actual realization is far less exciting.

*b.2.b.1. CALM ABIDING*

> **The waves of gross and subtle thoughts subside**
> **in their own place.**
> **The stream of mind rests unmoved in itself.**
> **May we be free from the stains of agitation, stu-**
> **por, and dullness,**
> **And establish a still ocean of calm abiding.**

This prayer describes the ideal state of calm abiding. In this state all gross and subtle thoughts are naturally pacified, which is to say that they are temporarily calmed down. When the mind is free from any disturbing thoughts, it becomes stable and abides in this state without there being any need for deliberate effort. In this situation two things can happen. The first is agitation (Tib. *jing wa*). This refers to an extroverted state in which the mind, figuratively speaking, falls into a gaze, in which it is very fascinated or "spaced out." The second consists of two types of an extremely introverted state of mind, stupor and dullness (Tib. *mug pa* and *nyog pa*). These are almost the same, though dullness is slightly more active, while under the influence of stupor one might easily fall asleep. It is a state of real blankness, while dullness is a state of extreme cloudiness that can be compared to water polluted by so much dirt that one cannot see through it.

When we achieve a state in which our mind is without agitation, stupor, or dullness, and when in addition to that it is naturally and effortlessly calm, free from any gross or subtle thoughts, this is the ideal state of calm abiding, which is comparable to a still ocean. This is what a *shi né* practitioner should achieve and what the Third Karmapa therefore prays for.

*b.2.b.2. SPECIAL INSIGHT*

> While looking again and again at the mind
>     which cannot be looked at,
> The meaning which cannot be seen is seen
>     vividly, just as it is.
> This cuts all doubts as to "this" and "not this"
>     with regard to the meaning.

**May we be free from delusion and thus recognize our own face.**

The purpose of practicing calm abiding is not just to relieve our stress, but to vividly see the nature of our mind. This is much more likely to happen in a calm state of mind; without the mind being calm it is almost impossible. To look at the mind means to observe it, though the mind is not something that can be visually perceived in the ordinary dualistic manner. While observing the mind we will see, realize, and feel what cannot be looked at and perceived in this way. At this point all our doubts as to whether or not this is the true nature of mind will dissolve. We therefore pray: May I see my own face, may I clearly recognize the nature of my mind.

Up to this point we have already covered quite an important part of this prayer. We have learned what is meant by meditation in general and by calm abiding and special insight in particular. In this context, it is very important to understand that we have to respect our present state of mind, our present level of consciousness, and that we have to acknowledge what we are able to do and not do for the time being, since otherwise our view, our action, and our meditation might conflict with each other. So we pray that we may gain the capacity of meditating without any deliberate effort, yet at the same time we have to exert every possible effort to achieve this aim. Therefore it would be very wrong to force or brainwash ourselves in order to be a person we are not as yet. To be aware of this is very important for anyone who is a serious practitioner. For philosophers this does not constitute a problem; they just study and talk. The same is true of anyone who is just a devotee. A practitioner, though, when gaining knowledge, thereby knows how he or she ought to be, and when the performance falls short such a person may fight and struggle hard inwardly in order to come up to the expectations. Yet by desperate endeavor nothing will be achieved. Therefore we have to cool down and relax, we have to accept the quality of our effort and also our shortcomings, and then to work on this basis. This is another example of what I meant by saying that we first need a structured ego.

### b.2.b.3. SEEING DURING THE POST-MEDITATIVE STATE

This prayer describes how everything in life is viewed in the vision of special insight.

> **When looking at an object, there is no object: it**
> **is seen as mind.**
> **When looking at the mind, there is no mind: it**
> **is empty of essence.**
> **When looking at both, dualistic fixation is freed**
> **of itself.**
> **May we realize clear light, the nature of our mind.**

The meaning of this verse is as follows: When looking at external objects we realize that they are manifestations of our own mind. When looking inward at the mind we see that it does not have any kind of true existence, it does not exist as a dualistic entity independent from others. When we then look at both, dualism just collapses. In this way we see our mind and its connection with everything else. This is what the Mahamudra teachings describe as "clear light" or as "luminosity" (Tib. *ö sel wa*): it is the characteristic of the mind, the way the mind exists. This means that everything we perceive as an object out there, and everything we hold to be the perceiving subject, is interdependent. There is no more and no less than interdependent manifestation. And the essence of the mind is clarity. It is not luminous like a source of light, but clear. This is the definition of the term "clear light." When the mind is seen it is clear. Somebody may be blind or live in total darkness, but when this person's mind is clear, everything is clear. To the mind there is no such thing as darkness or light, the nature of darkness and light being equally relative. This clarity is the definition of *ö sel wa*. It does not mean that the mind is a kind of light bulb. So we pray that we may see and realize this clear light.

*b.2.b.4. UNION OF CALM ABIDING AND SPECIAL INSIGHT*

> **Free from mental creation it is Mahamudra.**
> **Free from extremes it is Great Madhyamaka.**
> **Being all-inclusive it is also called Great**
> **Perfection.**
> **May we gain certainty that, by knowing one,**
> **all meanings are realized.**

This prayer contains the definitions of Mahamudra, Madhyamaka, and Maha Ati, the Great Perfection. Within the system of the Mahamudra the mind is shown to be beyond the bondage of thoughts and concepts. Thoughts and concepts are relative manifestations of the mind; they appear as long as the mind is not realized, but the mind itself is at all times free from this bondage. Its true nature is beyond any extreme. These extremes are mentioned in detail in the system of the Madhyamaka, which extensively classifies them into groups of four, of eight, and so forth. Simply speaking, though, both Mahamudra and Madhyamaka mean that the mind is beyond any limitation. Then again, everything that the Buddha has taught, Mahamudra and Madhyamaka as well as all the other teachings he has given, is about the nature of the mind, since the mind is the essence of everything. This is expressed within the system of the Great Perfection (Tib. *dzog pa chen po*). If we realize this, everything is accomplished. Thus the profound knowing of one thing will unfold the knowledge and wisdom of everything. We therefore pray that we may gain this insight.

*b.2.b.5. EXPERIENCE*

> **Uninterrupted great bliss free from attachment,**
> **Unobscured clear light free from fixation on characteristics,**
> **Spontaneous absence of thought beyond intellect:**
> **May these be experienced unceasingly without deliberate effort.**

This verse means the following: When some basic stability and clarity are present, this is accompanied by great joy without there being any attachment to it. At the same time there is the experience of clarity, of clear light, which is unobscured in that it does not involve subject and object. Just by seeing the nature of mind, it is seen as clarity. This experience of joy and clarity takes place without thought and deliberate effort and we pray that we may have this experience. When it happens, though, we might think that we are already enlightened, since it is definitely very exciting! But the moment excitement arises, there will also arise everything that the mind must be free from in order for the experience to happen. There will be attachment to the joy (Tib. *shen pa*), grasping to the characteristics of the object perceived (Tib. *tsen dzin*), conceptual mind (Tib. *lo*), deliberate effort (Tib. *bé tsol*), and all the rest. Then the actual experience has vanished in a haze and we are back to square one. Therefore we pray for an authentic experience that is free from these impediments.

*b.2.b.6. REALIZATION*

> May our desire for good meditation, our
>   clinging to experience, be liberated in its
>   own place.
> May the delusion of negative thoughts become
>   pure as the expanse of the nature [of mind].
> The ordinary mind is not to be obtained. There
>   is nothing to be adopted and nothing to be
>   abandoned.

**May we realize the truth of the dharmata, which
is free from any conceptual elaboration.**

This verse describes actual realization, the achievement
of the path. There are two obstacles that prevent realization. The first is attachment to meditation experience, the
wish for good experiences in meditation. Therefore we
pray that this obstacle may be self-liberated, which is to
say that one has to be freed from it effortlessly—one cannot remove it deliberately. The second consists of any kind
of negative thoughts. This refers to dualistic bondage as
such, which in its entirety is considered as being negative
since it constitutes a hindrance to realization; we therefore
have to free ourselves from any dualistic bondage. Realization itself is the recognition of ordinary mind. This
means that we have always had buddha nature, and it is
here with us now. Thus the definition of enlightenment is
the full realization and release of this potential of ultimate
freedom and liberation. So we wish for this true realization, this true achievement. We have to call it an achievement, since this is how our mind functions—there is a
goal that we reach. Nevertheless, when one has become a
buddha one will not think: "Now I have done it!" It is not
like a person having won a gold medal and jumping and
crying with joy. Reaching buddhahood is not achieving a
goal, though in the meantime we have to consider it in
those terms, since we have a structured ego.

*b.3. SUPPLICATIONS PERTAINING TO THE ACTION*

These consist of two prayers. The first describes compassion, and the second the union of compassion and emptiness.

*b.3.a. COMPASSION*

> **The nature of beings is always buddha.**
> **Yet, not realizing this, they wander through the**
> **endless cycle of existence.**
> **For all beings in their boundless suffering**
> **May intolerable compassion be born in our**
> **stream of being.**

The meaning of this verse is as follows: The nature or the essence of every sentient being is always buddha dharmakaya; solely due to the fact that they do not realize this, sentient beings wander through the realm of samsara. Samsara is endless suffering. For this reason we pray: May we develop limitless compassion, may it always be present within us.

Through this prayer, compassion is defined very clearly. Compassion does not mean having concern for someone because he or she has a headache. Compassion as it is described here means that every sentient being suffers unnecessarily—suffering is not the nature of sentient beings, it is not in accord with their potential. Their potential is buddha. Compassion is therefore respect for all sentient beings who are suffering although this potential is present within them. To depict this compassion the

Karmapa uses the Tibetan term *sö mé*, the literal meaning of which is "unbearable" or "intolerable." Once such compassion has arisen one cannot be patient with it, one cannot tolerate it. This is to say that all of us will definitely have compassion for all sentient beings who are less enlightened than we are, and this will happen naturally and spontaneously. It does not mean that we would feel desperately compelled to impose our ideas on other people or to chase after them in order to help them.

### b. 3. b. THE UNION OF COMPASSION AND EMPTINESS

> **Even as the skillful activity of intolerable**
> **compassion unfolds without hindrance,**
> **May the meaning of its empty essence at the**
> **same time nakedly shine forth.**
> **Inseparable from this supreme unerring path**
> **of union,**
> **May we meditate at all times, day and night.**

When the strong compassion described in the preceding prayer is present, and at the same time it is seen that its nature is beyond any limitation, this recognition is the realization of the union of compassion and emptiness. This constitutes a high level of realization, and once it is achieved our path cannot go amiss any more; there is no room for this to happen. We therefore pray: May this union of compassion and emptiness continuously manifest in all our actions. "Day and night" means continuously, uninterruptedly. When this state is reached, every action, every moment, is equally important. There are no longer any differences such as thinking: "Now I am meditating in my shrine-room," and thus behaving well, as opposed to thinking: "Now I'm on holiday," and becoming rather defiled. When the union of compassion and emptiness is reached, everything is of equal importance.

*E. FRUITION*

> **Developing the eyes and clairvoyant perception**
> **that arise from the power of meditation,**
> **May we ripen beings, purify buddha-fields,**
> **and perfect the wishing prayers**
> **That accomplish all the qualities of the Buddha.**
> **May we lead the three aspects of perfecting,**
> **ripening, and purifying to their ultimate**
> **level and attain buddhahood.**

The main part of this prayer describes the accomplishment reached by a great enlightened bodhisattva who is not yet a buddha. Only the last sentence refers to the state of buddhahood itself, describing it in a very profound way.

Through the power of meditation, which is to say as a result of our practice, we will attain a special capacity of sight and of mental clairvoyance. There are five types of "eyes" and six types of clairvoyance (Tib. *ngön shé*) through which one is able to perceive and know things that are taking place somewhere else, or that could normally not be perceived and understood, just as if they were happening where one is. If all of these were explained here, it could easily get confusing, and at the same time would not be very useful. As long as we do not have these capacities, it does not mean too much to have an intellectual knowledge of them, apart from enabling us to write a book and maybe getting an academic degree. I will therefore give just one example for each. Literally translated the first of the five types of "eye" is called "flesh-eye." This is attained by a bodhisattva who has reached the eighth bodhisattva-level, and allows him or her to see everything taking place within the entirety of one group of universes. One such group consists of one thousand solar systems, multiplied twice more by a thousand. The flesh-eye can see everything that happens in this whole sphere. It can see it according to the perception of a human, an animal, a spirit, a god—in every possible way. Of these, the ways in which humans see things are already beyond count. We are just one type, human beings of the planet earth within our galaxy, and beside us there are countless different kinds of human beings who see in correspondingly different ways. This is the limitation of the visual faculty of a bodhisattva who has reached the eighth bhumi.

One of the six types of clairvoyance is called "miracle clairvoyance," or "clairvoyance that enables one to perform miracles" (Tib. *dzu trül gyi ngön shé*). Once we have realized everything to be an illusion, we are increasingly able to perform anything. A bodhisattva who has reached the first bodhisattva-level, for instance, is capable of manifesting simultaneously in a hundred physical forms in a hundred different places and doing a hundred different things. For a bodhisattva on the second bodhisattva-level this capacity has multiplied by a hundred, and for a bodhisattva on the third level by another hundred. A buddha has no limitation.

The prayer then speaks of ripening beings, purifying buddha-fields, and perfecting the wishing prayers that accomplish the qualities of the Buddha. "Ripening" (Tib. *min pa*) refers to the capacity of leading sentient beings to maturation in the sense of their gaining a greater ability to understand, to cope with their reality and to have further realization. When the Karmapa speaks of "purifying buddha-fields," this should not be understood in the literal sense. The connection we have with buddha-fields comes about through visualization, initiation, and through taking part in certain types of mandalas. In contrast to this, the reality of the great bodhisattvas is that they can receive transmission directly from the sambhogakaya aspect of the Buddha. This is what the phrase "purifying buddha-fields" expresses: it is like going to the school of the buddhas.

In the last sentence the Karmapa prays that we may lead the three aspects of ripening, purifying (Tib. *jang wa*), and perfecting (Tib. *dzog pa*) to their ultimate level. This is another way of describing enlightenment, which is a state of completeness, the accomplishment of perfection, maturation, and purification. All sentient beings are buddha in potential. Enlightenment is perfection in the sense that every potential, every quality, has become fully mature and complete. Maturation means that first we ourselves have become totally ripened, that we have reached total maturity in accordance with our potential, which is buddha. Once we have become mature ourselves, we can lead others to maturation; our own maturation has to come first, otherwise we will not have this capacity. Purification means that all the qualities, all the transmissions of the Buddha, have to be revealed so that they manifest completely. When these three have reached their ultimate level, this is the manifestation of buddhahood.

## Part Three: Dedication

This contains the conclusion of the prayer, the dedication.

> **By the power of the compassion of the victorious**
> **ones of the ten directions and their sons,**
> **And by the power of every unstained virtue as**
> **much as there is,**
> **May these pure supplications of myself and all**
> **beings**
> **Reach fulfillment just as they are.**

In short, here the Karmapa prays: May my pure supplications and those of all sentient beings, everything that has been expressed in this prayer, come true through the blessing of the buddhas and bodhisattvas and through the power of all the good deeds we have done. Indirectly this indicates the fact that there is nothing the buddhas and bodhisattvas can do without there being virtuous actions. These again stem from the buddhas and bodhisattvas. This is the definition of the lineage. If, without there being the lineage, we wanted something truly good to happen, it would not come to pass. For this aim we need all the necessary conditions. This is what the Karmapa expresses as the conclusion of his prayer.

Finally, it could be beneficial to explain in more detail a few things that have been mentioned before. The first is compassion. The definition of compassion in light of the Mahayana or Vajrayana is very specific. Compassion in that sense has to be in accordance with the definition of what a sentient being is, and what suffering is from the point of view of the ultimate truth. In this way it is very profound. At the same time the sole aim of every Vajrayana Buddhist is to attain enlightenment. That is the characteristic of a Vajrayana Buddhist. For this reason the compassion of such a person should serve to reduce dualism, it should lead toward and bring sentient beings closer to enlightenment. This is the single motivation for having compassion or for doing something beneficial for others. Otherwise even a very good attitude such as compassion could create a further separation, a distance between ourselves and others.

The second point which might need some further explanation is the phrase "to purify buddha-fields" (Tib. *shing jang wa*), which is part of the preceding verse. This is best understood by a statement central to Vajrayana Buddhism: All victorious ones, all buddhas, are one within the field of primordial wisdom. This is to say that once we become a buddha we become inseparable from all buddhas. While we are a bodhisattva, though, we are not yet buddha. There is a separation. We need the transmission by means of which we will transform into a buddha and thus become inseparable from all buddhas. This is the meaning behind the expression "purifying buddha-fields." It does not mean that one travels through all the buddha-fields to collect information and get advice. It denotes the transformation of ourselves being separate from all the buddhas into being inseparable from them. This is another definition of enlightenment. It is impossible to be enlightened and still limited, calling oneself "Buddha So-and-So" and having a letterhead.

In this context one might wonder why it is said that all buddhas are inseparable in the field of primordial wisdom, while at the same time each is described as residing in a certain pure land, in a certain direction, and having a specific color such as white, green, yellow, and so forth. This does not mean that the buddhas themselves are limited to such things. It is not to be understood in the sense that the home of Buddha Ratnasambhava, for instance, is all yellow as opposed to another buddha's place of residence having another color. There are no specific territories allocated to each buddha. This way of description mirrors our connection with the buddhas. For us there is east, south, west, and north, and each of these directions has a particular meaning: it is not east and so forth for no reason. In the same way, each of our defilements such as attachment, anger, jealousy, and so forth has a specific representation of its pure aspect. This is what each buddha, each wisdom, and each pure land stands for. Thus the purification of buddha-fields is also part of the final transformation of each of our defilements and limitations. (For further information see the Appendix).

With this we have completed the Mahamudra prayer. I hope my transmission is in accordance with our profound lineage and there has been no omission or mistake; I did my best to convey it as I received it from my teachers. In this way I hope it will be beneficial for your knowledge, and especially for the cultivation of your practice.

the lineage will disappear. Then Buddhist activity will be
like looking for sunken ships. We will look for and discover Buddhist objects, and then do research upon them.
We will put them into laboratories to find out what they
are; we will read texts and try to interpret them in ten
thousand different ways. At this time something resem-
bling Buddhism would exist, but the real thing would
not be present any more, because of there being no lineage.

Yesterday I was asked a question that I found very interesting. The question was whether a German Buddhist
needed another kind of meditation, since Tibetans and
Germans have different cultures. If meditation was just
some kind of training, the answer would be yes, because
different people have to be trained for different things. If
meditation was like this, each country would have its own
specific type: there would be French, German, English,
and Tibetan meditations. Ultimately, the varieties would
be endless, with every single human being having a different type of meditation especially designed to suit his
or her particular needs. Meditation would then be like
clothing: because every person has a different hat size,
there are all kinds of hats, some small, some big, and so
forth.

It opens something in my mind when I am asked such
a question. The teaching of the Buddha is the lineage. To
design a different kind of meditation I would have to be
a buddha. If I am not enlightened, if I am not a buddha,

# Concluding Remarks

In closing, I would like to say a few words about an issue that is very meaningful to me: the preservation of the Buddha's teaching. First I would like to talk about the importance of the lineage. I personally feel that it is crucial to remember that it is our common duty to ensure the future of Lord Buddha's lineage. Sometimes it takes us a little while to see what the true definition of Buddhism is. There are Buddhist books, temples and centers, images of the Buddha, all kinds of things—yet real Buddhism is the teaching of the Buddha, the living instruction that has been passed on from master to disciple. If we are able to maintain and preserve this, Buddhism will be present for a very long time. If we fail, there may be thousands of Buddhist temples, but true Buddhism would not exist any longer.

The lineage is the definition of Buddhism; without lineage there is no Buddhism. If we are not aware of this, how could I make up a new meditation? If I did so I would simply be using my disciples. It would be like working in a laboratory, testing new medicines on guinea pigs.

The teaching of Lord Buddha is the manifestation of his realization. The Buddha is not a professor who goes to a library to study, then goes home to work out his lecture and reflect upon what to tell his disciples tomorrow. The teaching of the Buddha is not like this. The Buddha's realization has no limitation, and his teaching is the manifestation of this limitless realization. Saying it is a manifestation means that it is not a dualistic concept, it is not the Buddha's idea. The Buddha's teaching is part of his realization, manifesting like a sun manifests light and warmth. This is the source of our lineage.

So, no matter whether we are German, Indian, Chinese, Tibetan, or of any other nationality, the meditation, the teaching that we receive, has to be exactly the same as it was taught by the Buddha. There cannot be different styles of meditation—German, French, Tibetan, and so forth. I understand, though, that people ask such questions and I appreciate it. Someone like myself who has been taught, trained, and who received transmission since early childhood would never think about these things of his own accord, they are so obvious. I therefore find a question like this very helpful. It leads me to think and to reconfirm the definition of the lineage. The instructions and the lineage have to accord with the teaching of the Buddha.

There cannot be any adjustment. Yet the Buddha has given so many methods that there are enough for all individuals. These methods have to be taught and received in accordance with the lineage, and within this framework each person can be given a method that corresponds best to his or her individual state of mind. We cannot make up a new method, though. If I could do so, I would most certainly wear a three-piece suit rather than my Tibetan robes. They look far too strange! Of course, the lineage does not depend upon the outer appearance too much; the teaching, the blessing, and the transmission come from the Buddha—they do not stem from the ideas of somebody like me. If my disciples thought so they would be in big trouble! When they understand that my teaching comes from the Buddha, that the instruction they receive from me is the teaching of the Buddha that I received, this view is absolutely correct. They are the followers of the Buddha through me, through their guru, but they are not my followers without the Buddha. To understand this is very important.

I am aware that sometimes I sound extremely conservative. In this respect someone who listens to me should relax and not get over-worried. There is no need to be too conservative. We should see the importance of preserving the lineage, but at the same time we should relax. Each of us has so many things to work out, and we can only do so when we are able to breathe normally. If we worry too much about this and that, it can become a personal hindrance. The task of worrying is maybe my karma. I think, in some ways, people like me have to bear this responsibility, along with the honor it contains. We do our best to preserve the lineage and our disciples have to realize their share of the responsibility. Yet this responsibility is fulfilled to a very large extent by practicing whatever they have learned from their teacher, and by doing their best.

The outer appearance—the robes, the rituals, and so forth—will transform slowly. Slow transformation is allowed. The Buddha himself said that the essence has to remain pure, whereas the ways in which it is presented can gradually and naturally transform. But they cannot be changed intentionally. If we started thinking: "I am going to do it this way, then many people will come; if I do it the other way, very few will come," we might end up wanting to change everything. "Let's dance the prayer!" This would not be a very good approach. Yet, if slowly, slowly first the prayer was chanted in melodies for maybe ten years, then people started moving for another ten years, then danced a bit, this would be fine. This would be similar to evolution. It would happen naturally, not out of ego. It would not involve greed and fear. In this way even the robes we Tibetans wear are quite different from those the Indian masters wore during the time of the Buddha. According to the teachings of the Buddha, one of the colors that monks and nuns are allowed to wear is blue, yet if a Tibetan monk decided to wear blue robes, he would be considered to be a follower of the Bön tradition—as a Buddhist, one is supposed to wear maroon. There is nothing wrong with Bön, it is almost identical to Buddhism, but one would be believed to be the follower of a completely different lineage. So if I wore blue robes tomorrow exactly in accordance with the Buddha's words, it would be a scandal. People would say, "The Tai Situpa has become a Bönpo!" Thus everything has to evolve slowly.

When we look at Chinese, Japanese, or Korean Buddhists they look totally different from Indian, Thai, or Tibetan Buddhists. These differences emerged over centuries. Twenty-five hundred years is a long time. This perspective opens ample space for us to be flexible. There is therefore no need to worry too much: I am sometimes a bit too conservative.

Nevertheless, as I said earlier, I feel very encouraged and inspired when I come to places such as this, since the people are really able to understand the Dharma, and many practice it very seriously. In this way, the continuation of our lineage is evident. Furthermore, when our great teachers come to such a center, it creates an opportunity for people who like to study and practice. Thus a tremendous and natural propagation of the Dharma takes place.

This is another topic regarding which I am slightly extreme. I do not believe very much in propagation. I believe in preservation. Once the pure teaching is preserved and the lineage is present, people can feel this. When the authentic teaching of the Dharma is preserved and practiced, it is like the sun, which from the very moment it rises everybody can see, everybody can feel, and everybody can benefit from. This is why I believe in preservation: preservation itself will propagate the Dharma, and will do so naturally. I am not against missionaries, but if Buddhists adopted their style, I would worry. If that happened, I would deem it to be the end of Buddhism. If I tried to go around and win people over and gather them around me, it would be awful! It could also be called a U.F.E.: an unidentified flying ego. Still, whenever someone appreciates the Dharma and wants to learn, we should not hesitate. We should provide the necessary conditions: we should open centers and do anything we can.

It is very important to keep these issues in mind, especially now that Vajrayana Buddhism is growing to such an extent. If we do not think carefully about these things, if we are not concerned with preservation, we might simply become propagators, the heads of some institution. This would be the beginning of the end. Thus this subject is very important, though again it is primarily the task of the teachers. Yet the disciples have to play their part, and for this reason I mention it.

# Questions and Answers

*Question:* So we should have a clear view of an "I," of an ego?

*Answer:* We should definitely have it loudly and clearly! Otherwise our guru would find himself forced to introduce the ego before being able to introduce buddha nature. This would be an extra job for him! The ego job should be done by ourselves. The purpose of the Dharma is to lead us to see the non-existence of an ego in terms of a dualistic entity, and to see ourselves as buddha, as being limitless and perfect. Therefore, if we do not clearly see this ego within ourselves, it is not positive. In my view it is negative when a person is not firm and clear in this respect; it causes extra work. If a person does not have an ego, this is very good. But usually there is actually a very big ego that is not seen or admitted. If such a person says: "I have no ego!" and somebody opposes this and says: "Yes, you have," the argument goes back and forth until the person devoid of ego says: "If you don't stop now and believe me, I will call the police!" No ego! Then this person might write a voluminous book about non-ego, make a big painting or sculpture of non-ego, or build a museum for it. It is very difficult to work this out. So, I think, to first see our own ego very clearly, to recognize and accept it, is a very good foundation. In this way Dharma practice can really dissolve into a person.

*Question:* I am a little bit surprised that the Third Karmapa is so very humble.

*Answer:* To be humble is very good. Sometimes people say that it is not honest to be humble. I disagree completely. In my view this is an excuse to assert our ego. Being as humble as possible is very good: it is not a lie. We should be as humble as we can, not in a depressed way, but happily humble. To be uptight and upset and miserably humble is of no avail, but to be happy, uplifted, full of confidence, and at the same time humble is very good. It is also not very difficult. There is no sacrifice involved, it does not constitute a loss. We only gain when we are humble.

*Question:* You said that a positive action alone is not enough, but should be carried out in accordance with the Mahayana principle. Could you give an example of this?

*Answer:* It is definitely good enough, but not good enough to become a condition that leads us to enlightenment. Apart from that, every positive action is good enough. Even giving half of an apple to someone who has nothing to eat, or throwing leftover bread into a bush for the birds and insects is very good. Yet whether or not this kind of activity will become a condition leading to enlightenment depends upon the Mahayana principle. It depends on bodhichitta. If we have developed bodhichitta and do good deeds with this motivation, our actions become a condition that will bring us closer to realization. If we think: "I give this in order to accumulate merit and thus attain enlightenment for the benefit of all sentient beings," if this is our purpose of living, the reason behind our actions, we directly follow the path to enlightenment. It is of course impossible to consciously bring this to mind each time we make a little move, but if this motivation has become our principle, we will eventually reach complete enlightenment.

There is another type of realization that does not constitute complete enlightenment. This is sometimes described by the Sanskrit term "nirvana." It is a state of freedom from suffering in which all thoughts, all emotions and defilements are completely exhausted so that one has become totally pure; yet at the same time it is a state of total extinction in which everything has ceased,

everything has gone to zero. This is not the complete enlightenment that the Mahayana and Vajrayana aim at. The
Karmapa describes the particular merit necessary to reach
this complete realization.

*Question:* Buddha Shakyamuni had a human form. Will
this also be true of the future Buddha Maitreya?

*Answer:* He will be the son of his father and mother just
like Buddha Shakyamuni was. It is prophesied that all
the thousand buddhas will appear in such a form.

*Question:* How can we ensure that we will be there twenty
thousand centuries from now?

*Answer:* There is no need to worry. There are only two
possibilities. We will either be there as a sentient being or
as a buddha—as a buddha to bless him or as a sentient
being to receive him.

*Question:* The Buddha will be the son of his father and
mother, not their daughter?

*Answer:* As I said already, for a woman to talk too nega-
tively about men and take advantage of them is also bad
karma. The same is true of a man who talks too nega-
tively about women and takes advantage of them. If one
attacks men or women, this is equally bad karma. Yet I
can understand the women's way of thinking. This way
of thinking is not negative; in my view it is good. When it

goes too far, though, it could become quite unnatural; apart from that I think it is right. If certain people have taken advantage of others for a very long time, they will have to pay the price. This is not something negative. At times there has to be a raising of consciousness, as has been the case, for instance, with regard to ecological problems. For a long time the environment has just been exploited, but nowadays many people are conscious of this, are more careful, more considerate and concerned about the welfare of the future generations. I think this is wonderful; the same can be said for becoming conscious of the oppression of women through men. When something is going too far somebody has to stand up and say something, otherwise everybody will just follow the crowd so that nothing changes. In this way, so many people will suffer, which is not only unnecessary but negative. The Buddhist view of this is very clear. There are so many female Buddhas and the Buddha has pointed out unmistakably that every sentient being is equal to the Buddha. In certain texts, though, one may find some statements that seem to indicate the opposite, but I think these could be due to concepts popular at the time.

*Question:* You spoke about the unclear ego and pointed out that it was necessary to free ourselves from our confusion with regard to the ego in order to be able to work with it. Could you give some general advice how to do this?

*Answer:* We should be more practical, more realistic, more down to earth, and be skillful in living our lives. Then we will be a canvas on which a good painting can be made. This has to be worked out first. The answer to the question whether or not a human being is able to do so is another way of determining the difference between a mature and a not yet settled person. A mature person has his or her thoughts and actions together.

*Question:* How can we integrate the practice of Dharma into our daily routine, into our profession, our family life, and so forth?

*Answer:* We have to transform our ordinary life into practice, since for a Vajrayana Buddhist the sole purpose of living and of doing anything is to attain liberation in order to benefit all sentient beings. If this is not our motivation, we are not Vajrayana Buddhists. With this motivation we try to do our duty, everything that needs to be done, with as much mindfulness and awareness as possible. Yet in doing so we should not get too obsessed, not even by good things. Being too fixated, we become blinded, our vision loses any sense of proportion; if we focus on something too firmly and closely we will only see this particular item and nothing else. When I hold my thumb in front of my eyes, at first I will know it to be my thumb, but if I continued doing so I might not remember this any longer; I might think that my thumb was bigger than the whole world. Taking it a bit further away I will see its actual size. If we hold on to something too much, worry too much, this can become a real problem. We might end up not knowing how to do things we already knew how to do. When the Third Karmapa describes in this prayer the union of emptiness and compassion, in my view this constitutes a very profound way to make it work. At the same time we truly have to understand that everything is related to everything else; thus some kinds of work could be more positive than others, but after all everything is connected. This fact provides the ways and means to transform anything. Some things are difficult to transform, others are easier. This depends totally upon the level of maturity each of us has reached.

*Question:* When speaking of "view, meditation, and action" and also about "ground, path, and fruition," are these to be understood as being synonymous, or, if otherwise, what is the connection between them?

*Answer:* One can make a connection, of course, but meditation and action actually constitute the path. One could consider the view as being the ground. Yet this would be the view of the ground. There is also a view of the path and of the fruition. View refers to the way we think, to our philosophy, to Mahamudra philosophy. Path is meditation and action. As for the view, we can have a view of the fruition, of the path, and the ground, as well as of everything else.

*Question: :* The definition of Mahamudra is to be able to rest in the nature of mind. This is what I understood from the preceding teachings. I also understood that this is almost equivalent to the state of buddhahood. How can I discern the difference between resting in the nature of my mind or just having a certain amount of tranquillity as is achieved once my practice of calm abiding has become stable or once I have received oral instructions on Mahamudra?

*Answer:* Resting in the nature of mind is one type of Mahamudra practice. Although this constitutes an essential aspect, Mahamudra practice is not limited to it, but covers everything. If, for instance, we contemplate the preciousness of human life, or if we contemplate death, impermanence, and so forth, these are also Mahamudra practices, in the sense of being preliminary practices. The ability to rest in the nature of our mind represents an advanced level that is not very far from realization. Someone with this ability may not necessarily be enlightened, but such a person is nearing the point at which realization takes place.

When we have reached a good state of calm abiding and special insight we will definitely know that. Yet this is where we need a master and a lineage. The task of the master is to teach the disciple everything that he or she has to know and practice and to see which level of realization the disciple has reached. For this reason we need a guru; this is what a guru is for.

*Question:* I often wonder what is wrong with our understanding of the Dharma, in that I frequently see people who practice but who become more confused, more jealous, and more proud, especially when they have a position in a Dharma center or are very close to a high lama. In this case they are more proud and jealous and try to protect this teacher claiming him to be their very own while others have to stay out. Therefore, what is wrong with the practice or what can we do about this?

*Answer:* I think there is nothing wrong. Until we reach a certain level the defilements will be there. Within the practice of the Mahayana there are five paths. The second of these consists of three stages called patience, heat, and peak (Tib. *sö pa, drö,* and *tsé mo*). The stage of patience constitutes a particular state or level of realization, and until we have reached this state we will have all the defilements. I do not think that everybody who practices the Dharma will get proud, jealous, and so forth, though definitely a weaker person might fall into all of that. This does not mean there is something wrong; it just means that this person has not yet gained realization and is not enlightened. It is also not necessarily due to being close to a high lama. We can see many serious practitioners who, without being close to a high teacher, complete some amount of retreat or practice and thereupon develop a certain kind of negativity. Then again there are others who have practiced for many years, who are very learned and good people, and yet at the same time are very humble and sincere. Therefore the process you described will not inevitably happen. I do not think that every Westerner is allergic to realization, but I can understand your point!

In this context it should also be taken into account that among Buddhists in the West, everybody practices. Of course, this is not true of one hundred percent but almost everybody meditates, practices a sadhana and so forth, and thus makes a genuine effort toward the actual purpose. In Tibet everybody recited mantras and prayed. This type of practice would be common to all people. When it came to meditation, though, this was different, not everybody would know how to do it. This is a generalization, of course, and as such cannot be totally accurate. But I think there is no reason for you to worry. You do not like to be jealous and so forth and this is extremely good. We should not become more proud and confused in the course of our Dharma practice, but when it happens, I am afraid this just means that the person in question is not yet mature. It is quite all right. It will be all right in the long run. Furthermore, there is another aspect to be taken into account: although a person might not appear to be proud and so forth on the outside, nevertheless all these things might take place inside. For me as a teacher, my task is far easier when I can see them arise. Of course, there should not be an unreasonable outbreak, but when the manifestation is reasonable the teacher is able to see it and in consequence do something about it.

As for people who seem to get more confused once they practice more intensively, I have commented on this in some detail already. Everybody has an ego, everybody has ignorance. Yet in the West, and this is very much true of modern society, people are able to play a game. Somewhere back there in their minds, in a rather clever way, they manage to make themselves believe that they do not have an ego, that they are not like that. This makes everything very tricky. For this reason I said earlier that it is much better to have a structured ego rather than a U.F.O., an unidentified object; in the latter case the ego is there but is not identified as such. Although the ego is the same it is very difficult to deal with. The disciple would say: "I have no ego!" Then the teacher would say: "Oh yes you have!" and the disciple would deny it and in consequence say: "I am going to quit," or would call the police!

*Question:* My question concerns karma. As far as I understand it, we are meant to develop compassion not only for innocent victims but also for evildoers, since they are ignorant. On the other hand, I do not know whether I have understood this rightly, since it is said that karma cannot be changed, not even by a buddha. Why then do we pray with compassion for beings who have a more negative karma? Does this have any effect? Is the effect greater when such a being has just died, or is there also an effect during his or her lifetime?

*Answer:* This is a very good question. In this context we should understand that Buddhism accepts the existence of karma as being a relative truth. On the level of the ultimate truth, Buddhism does not believe in karma. Any good karma can be destroyed by negative karma and any negative karma can be destroyed by good karma. Both can be transformed through realization. Thus karma is not ultimate; it is a relative truth. As long as we are subject to duality, karma is the ruling power that determines everything that happens to us, yet since it is not ultimate it can be overcome by anything; praying for evil people also works on this basis. If karma was ultimate, you would be right: praying for others or doing something good would be really stupid, since everything would be predestined, thus there would be no point in trying to do something about it. While on the ultimate level karma does not mean anything, relatively speaking everything is karma.

Karma is nothing else than cause and condition, which is to say everything that happens is the result of its very own causes and conditions. These are of all kinds, and the way they act together is very complicated. There are countless karmas for every single little thing. Each hair that grows on my head has its own reason: the fact that it is thick, thin, black or white and so on is due to its individual causes and conditions. This process reaches back into the past forever. This is the definition of karma. Nothing happens out of nothing. Ultimately, though, nothing ever happened and nothing is happening. Thus, once we attain enlightenment, by definition, any karma we have is purified. If karma were really existent, we could give up the idea of wanting to reach enlightenment. There would be no way, since it might take millions of lives to purify the karma of one single day of living.

Some time ago I went for a walk in a place in France which was very nice but full of midges so tiny that one could easily breathe them in. While I was walking on the grass this set me thinking: that morning I had brushed my teeth; how many germs had been killed in this process? Maybe a million. Later that day I had eaten rice and meat and vegetables. How many animals were killed to grow each grain of rice I ate? How many insects and ants were drowned in the water, how many were poisoned by insecticides? Each grain of rice is produced at the cost of ten lives or maybe even a hundred lives: I ate a plateful of rice. Then the bread and the meat. The animal did not come to give the meat to me; somebody killed it. As for the vegetables, there would not be any unless all the insects and germs who would otherwise eat them were killed. Since we want to eat vegetables, the people who grow them have to get rid of all these animals. Then I drank water. If one really looks into water, it is full of life: thus drinking water is drinking liquid life. Then I walked on the grass. How many small beings got squashed? It is comparable to a giant walking over a big city. How many tiny bugs became orphans? All of these things are real. How many lives would it take to purify the karma of one day, if enlightenment took place by purifying each and every karma eye for eye? Enlightenment would be impossible.

Ultimately, though, we can never create a negative karma. Killing and stealing, for instance, exist as long as there is duality. Otherwise there is no killing and stealing. One can only kill the body, no one can kill the mind. Thus ultimately karma does not exist, although relatively everything is karma. A spot that has been in utter darkness for millions of centuries, that has not seen any light throughout all this time, does not need millions of centuries to become bright: the moment a light shines upon it it will be illuminated. Likewise, if we realize our ultimate essence, our ultimate nature, we will be enlightened and thus will have purified all the negativity of all our lifetimes. The reason why in Buddhism we pray for bad or good people, why we try to do positive things and avoid negative actions, is to facilitate this realization. If we do not discipline ourselves, we do so many unnecessary negative things. In order to tame ourselves, we take some vows and adopt a certain discipline. In doing so, again we should not worry too much: if we always worry, we will not even be able to drink a glass of water. We should avoid everything that is unnecessary, but at the same time we have to do whatever is necessary, such as drinking water, brushing our teeth, eating rice, and so forth. We do not have to kill any sentient being intentionally, and we do not have to steal from or cheat anybody; this is unnecessary negativity. We can reach enlightenment through realization only and not by merely doing good things. We do good things to help others temporarily, and to accumulate merit temporarily; this creates the conditions for us to be able to meditate, to pray, and to cultivate whatever is conducive to realization. Without this we would not even have these good conditions. In this way our path is directed toward enlightenment.

Thus karma is there, everything is karma, but only in the sense of a relative truth. As long as we call ourselves "I," we are under the total control of karma. Yet as soon as we become free from our limitations, as soon as we realize our ultimate limitless nature, we are liberated from all karma.

People in the West have one problem. They cannot bridge paradoxes. This ability is needed, otherwise one will never understand the ultimate truth; one will just be stuck in the relativity of the relative truth. Reality is not just of one kind, it is of all kinds; therefore, in order to understand reality, we have to be able to bridge paradoxes: the ultimate and the relative truth with regard to karma is quite a serious one. We cannot use our regular one-way concept to understand this; we have to go beyond it, one step further or deeper.

# Dedicating the Merit

I would like to dedicate the merit of the spiritual head of this center and of all the people who put their effort into making it a reality. For this course I have been requested to teach on Mahamudra. In this way we participated in the lineage of the Mahamudra prayer by the Third Gyalwa Karmapa and the lineage of the commentary written by the Eighth Tai Situpa. Thus we dedicate the merit that has arisen from this teaching as well as the merit of everybody who worked hard to make this course possible.

We dedicate this merit generally to all sentient beings so that they may attain enlightenment, and specifically to our planet earth. We pray that all the manifold problems that the human race is facing—all the wars, fighting, and other conflicts—may be clarified and that sentient beings may overcome all their sufferings. Furthermore we dedicate to all religions. Each religion, no matter what kind it is, is good for people as long as it is not misused.

We therefore pray that all religions may flourish for the benefit of all sentient beings. Then we dedicate to all Buddhists. There are many millions of Buddhists in this world. We pray that their connection with Lord Buddha and his teaching may be fruitful, and that they may be able to draw utmost benefit from his blessing and instruction. We particularly dedicate to Vajrayana Buddhism, to His Holiness the Dalai Lama, who is the head of all the Vajrayana schools, and to all the great masters of every Buddhist denomination. We especially dedicate to His Holiness the Seventeenth Gyalwa Karmapa, Urgyen Thrinlé Dorjé, the supreme leader of our lineage. Thus we dedicate to all the great masters, and wholeheartedly pray that they may have good health, a long life, and profound success in all their noble activities which they enact in the service of Lord Buddha for the benefit of all sentient beings. Then we dedicate the merit to all of our masters who are not with us at the moment. We pray that their incarnations may come soon to continue the activities of their previous incarnations, that there may be no obstacle to their return and that everything may be auspicious. Finally I dedicate all my merit to all of those who participated in this teaching. May their Dharma activities, their study and practice, be of great success. May they gain the best possible maturity through the profound teachings of the Buddha, and may everything be auspicious for all.

*Appendix*

The following is an authorized translation of two oral teachings given by the XII Khentin Tai Situpa in Berlin during his visit to Germany in 1986. The first contains more detailed explanations of the meaning of the terms "eternalism and nihilism" and "assertion and denial" and the second explains the five buddha families. These may add to the understanding of the preceding teachings.

# Mahamudra

Mahamudra is a term particularly used in the Karma Kagyü lineage as it covers everything within the Buddhist perspective. As such it is a vast subject. For a brief but thorough explanation, it can be structured as follows:

1. The meaning of the term Mahamudra
2. The subject itself presented as three phases:
   a. Ground Mahamudra, or basic, potential Mahamudra
   b. Path Mahamudra, or Mahamudra practice
   c. Fruition Mahamudra, or the result of Mahamudra practice

1. The term "Mahamudra" consists of two Sanskrit words. "Maha" means "great." The translation of "mudra" is slightly more difficult. It can stand for "gesture," for "seal," or for "symbol." Thus Mahamudra is "the great gesture," "the great seal," or "the great symbol."

Based upon this direct translation, the term can be explained as follows:

> Every aspect of reality is the gesture of the
> absolute truth.
> Every part of relative existence bears the seal of
> the absolute truth.
> Every relative manifestation is the symbol of
> the absolute truth.

These three are synonymous in that they lead to one conclusion. Within everything and about everything is an absolute potential. If we understand one thing correctly, we understand everything. Therefore "mudra" is both a simple and a comprehensive title, which could be said to be the heart of the Karma Kagyü lineage. This title or lineage covers everything, from the simplest common-sense idea such as: "If you eat food, your body will survive; if you eat poison, your body will die," up to the highest reality. It comprises the entire range of practitioners, from beginners, to those who are a little advanced, up to those who are further or fully advanced. Therefore it is called "maha" or "great."

2.*a.* Relating to reality from the Mahamudra point of view, it can be said that through the philosophy and concept of Mahamudra we are introduced to the value of ourselves and everything that is around us. We may view ourselves as capable or incapable, happy or sad. We may view the things around us as nice, passable, or quite bad. Yet, regardless of the way things appear, there is a depth within ourselves and the things around us—more than is seen superficially. Thus the basic view of Mahamudra philosophy prevents both overestimation and underestimation, providing a simple perspective that enables us to evaluate ourselves and the things around us without any such exaggeration.

To adopt this view we have to overcome eternalism and nihilism. This is strongly emphasized in the explanations of the basic Mahamudra principle. To avoid falling into either extreme, balance is needed, which is provided by the understanding of the relative and the absolute truths. This forms the basis of the development of an understanding of Mahamudra.

The balance resulting from the understanding of the relative and the absolute truths is therefore the first step in establishing the *view*, the *ground*, or the *foundation*. The view is the foundation, the foundation is the view. Whatever action we take in this world is always directly related to our view. Our view determines whether improvement takes place or the opposite. Therefore the view is the ground.

The proper view of the relative truth overcomes eternalism. This understanding of the relative truth is a very important point within Mahamudra philosophy, since according to this philosophy everything—from the smallest to the biggest, from the simplest to the most complicated—is part of the relative truth. This relativity, or in other words, the way in which everything appears, can prove to be quite detailed.

Using the example of a human being, one finds that all the constituents of a person (physical health, mental condition, psychological patterns) are in their entirety nothing but interdependent manifestations. Every process, every function, happens interdependently. A medicine which for one person has healing properties may be poisonous to another. What we do not know today we may know tomorrow. There is no more reality to it than interdependence. Everything is no more and no less than an interdependent manifestation.

Suppose that three people are exposed to an equally negative, extremely difficult situation. The first may not be able to deal with it. Overwhelmed by the difficulties he or she has to face, the person may go crazy or even commit suicide. The second will find it very hard, but learns from it, grows from it, and finally, with a great effort, survives. The third might not be affected by the negativity of the situation at all, but find it rather amusing and interesting.

Which of these three completely different experiences is reality? For each person his or her experience is real. There is a chance for each to enter into any of these realities, and this chance will occur through interdependence. In the relative sense everything is due to interdependence. This is the relative truth. The understanding of this interdependent origination, or the relative truth, overcomes eternalism, the belief in independent existence.

Falling into eternalism must be avoided, since with this view everything becomes so serious. One may become like the walking dead or like a robot, no longer able to adjust. Being completely fixed and narrow one is likely to be dangerous to oneself and to others. In this state of complete fixation a person is not far from being a corpse, since there is a total lack of openness, flexibility, and creativity. In this state the functioning of the mind is comparable to a gun barrel. This is the outcome of an eternalistic view.

The opposite extreme is nihilism. Its effect is quite similar to that of eternalism. Again this view provokes a state of complete lifelessness which denies the fact that there is more to a human being than he or she can see or feel. Someone may ask: "Do you believe in mind?" This is very interesting, in that it leads into a further question: "Who asks whether you believe in mind? Who wants to know whether there is such a thing as mind?" This shows that there is no need to think twice in order to know that there is more to it than our superficial knowledge. This is not complicated or fantastic. It is quite ordinary and obvious. Every human being has a potential to know everything, to improve through knowledge and realization. This improvement is not limited, but can continue until it reaches its summit, enlightenment. The process may take time, it is not just a weekend's job, but it will happen in time through doing what is right. This potential is there and is simple evidence that a human being is not just a vegetable.

Falling into nihilism, or denying one's potential, one gets totally disrespectful toward oneself. This view will lead to a state in which one neglects and wastes oneself one hundred percent. This is the result of nihilism.

Knowing that there is more to it than conventional knowledge admits, we have a fair chance to overcome nihilism. That is the absolute truth.

The relative truth always exists in accordance with something else. For a cow, grass is delicious food, but not for a human being. For a monkey a branch is a comfortable bed, but not for a human being. Yet about all these relative truths there is something further, in the sense that the absolute truth goes beyond the truth of the cow, the truth of the monkey, and the truth of the human being. It transcends everything that is a relative truth.

The attainment reached by the Buddha is usually described as "enlightenment." There is reason for hesitation, however, in using this term. Someone may ask: "Can you enlighten me?" Or, one may be handed a photograph of a smiling individual, and be given the explanation that this was taken at the moment of this person's enlightenment. In this way the word has become cheap. People may even ask whether they are enlightened. If this were the case they would know! Thus the question in itself is evidence that this enlightenment is to be doubted. In connection with the term "enlightenment," therefore, a certain cheapness is involved, together with the danger of misinterpretation and wrong connotations coming into play.

Nevertheless, the Buddha definitely attained a final realization or enlightenment that every human being is able to attain: the final ultimate state of consciousness which is the absolute truth. This will be attained through knowing the value of ourselves, of others, and of everything that is around us, as the potential for this final realization.

This is the view or the foundation, which constitutes the most important requirement in order to be able to progress on the path.

*2.b.*The fact that we have the potential and also the proper understanding is not sufficient. As long as this potential and understanding are not used, they might as well not be present. The proper use of our understanding, therefore, constitutes the *path* or the *practice*.

We have to use our time, every minute of it, as beneficially as possible. In doing so, whatever action we take—be it physical, verbal, or mental—has to follow our principle, our view, which should be free from eternalism and nihilism.

In the beginning the attempt is not altogether easy, and will lead us into situations that are comparable to the quick changes in fashions. One season brightly colored clothes may be promoted and soon everyone dresses accordingly and the whole town looks like a garden. The next season bright colors may be out, no-color declared the new fashion, and soon the whole town looks like the image of winter. In this situation again balance is needed; to provide this balance, it is emphasized in the explanations concerning the path that we have to be mindful not to assert and not to deny. Both are to be avoided, since assertion leads us into fanaticism, whereas denial causes us to waste our time.

This can be illustrated by means of a simple example, based on the maxim that one should not lie: A strong man attacks a weaker man and attempts to kill him with a knife. You see the weaker man run for his life and manage to hide in a nearby house. The strong man arrives in search of his victim and asks if you saw where he went. Being fanatically truthful you direct the strong man to the hiding place, with the result that the weaker man is killed, whereas a harmless lie would have saved his life. On the other hand, through lack of mindfulness our acceptance of lying may grow and finally go too far: we turn into someone who denies the validity of the relative truth, who lies and deceives and to whom even killing and stealing eventually seem permissible. Therefore, we should be constantly mindful not to fall into either of the extremes of fanaticism or carelessness.

If we are able to keep this balance, every aspect of our practice will continue to become more effective, with the dual aspects of purification and accumulation. We overcome all negativity and thus accumulate whatever is positive, meaningful, and beneficial. In this way total purification is total accumulation and total accumulation is total purification; their completeness is realization.

If purification and accumulation are carried out successfully, we are successful practitioners, in that we are able to make the best of our time. We improve and gradually gain the capacity to help others. As long as we cannot see, we cannot show the way to others. If we see a little, we can show a little. If we see in a wrong way, we may also show the wrong way. In short, good balance provides success, the ability to achieve greater improvement within a short time.

*2.c. Fruition* is not something that happens with a bang but is a continuous step-by-step process, the ultimate end of which is enlightenment. Today's practice is tomorrow's fruition. Fruition takes place gradually, first as the development of an ordinary being, until the higher level of consciousness is reached. During the process of this development there is always the risk of falling back, of getting contaminated or corrupted; once the higher level of consciousness is reached this is unlikely to occur. From this level onward one progresses through several stages of realization, the highest being that of a buddha. The higher level of consciousness is, for example, represented by the bodhisattvas such as Tara, Avalokiteshvara, or Manjushri. Once this level is attained one travels quite smoothly, as on a well-kept highway, whereas ordinary beings still use an unfinished road.

To describe the levels through which fruition takes place, four terms are used within the Mahamudra context: *One-pointedness* is reached when one is able to see the absolute truth within everything, including oneself. Making use of this ability, one goes beyond complication and reaches *non-complication*. On this level everything gets very easy—there is nothing one cannot manage. When one has grown familiar with non-complication and goes beyond it, everything is of *one taste*. Everything is the manifestation of the ultimate truth. On this level one has almost reached the goal, Mahamudra. Duality is almost transcended and there is the sense of sameness and equality. The fourth level is called *non-meditation*. This goes beyond effort. During the process of fruition, first a great amount of deliberate effort is needed, then a far smaller amount, then none. First it becomes; then one becomes; at this level it gets effortless.

The term "Mahamudra" is often misinterpreted as solely denoting a certain type of practice, by means of which one directly deals with the mind without further elaborations such as visualization and the recitation of prayers. Although this is considered a specialty of Mahamudra practice, the term is not limited to that, but covers far more. It involves the continuous presence of a sense of mindfulness, awareness, and connection with our basic nature, which is neither solid nor blank. This basic nature is within everything. It has the sense of voidness, and at the same time clarity. It has ultimate intelligence beyond eternalism and nihilism. It cannot be restricted to any extreme.

Sometimes this sense of clarity, voidness, and intelligence manifests in the form of devotion and compassion. It flashes like a shaft of lightning in darkest night, and for a moment we see more brightly. If we are carried away, taken over by our emotions, then this inspiration by which we have been touched will dry out, like the few tears that have fallen on our cheeks. Therefore it should be recognized as the manifestation of devotion and compassion.

# The Five Buddha Families

The Tibetan term *gyal wa rig nga* is usually translated as "the five buddha families." This title has a somewhat peculiar connotation, suggesting the image of a small village that consists of just five families. The translation seems quite accurate, though, and there is no better alternative.

The concept of the five buddha families reflects the basic principle of Buddhism. However, there is more emphasis on it within the Vajrayana system of teaching. There is no specific emphasis in the Hinayana or the Mahayana contexts, whereas in the Vajrayana it is described in detail. One should therefore consider this particular description to be a Vajrayana teaching, which will consequently involve a certain number of terms and concepts belonging only to the Vajrayana system.

Generally speaking, this particular aspect of teaching provides the sense of a clear connection of everything with everything else, in that it encompasses the source, or the actual center, as well as whatever manifests outside of this center. This is the mandala principle.

The term "mandala" nowadays is used for any kind of colorful pattern. Someone may drop a brush on a canvas and call the result a mandala. This term, however, is not just a fancy word, but holds both depth and potential. It literally translates as "center and surroundings." Thus it conveys the sense of manifestation from and absorption by the center.

Everything that exists does not just happen. It occurs as the simultaneous process of manifestation and absorption taking place within time, space, and concept, as well as beyond these. As such, the mandala principle describes a rather deep way of relating with ourselves and with everything that is out there.

In order to understand this principle, specific laws and rules must be taken into account, just as one needs four sides to describe a square, or three points to describe a triangle. When these laws and rules were expressed within the Vajrayana system, the five buddha families turned out to be the key to the mandala.

Often words in a foreign language are used without fully understanding them. Someone who does not know English very well may unwittingly call the person who cleans the bathroom "the president." Likewise, a painter may drop a brush and call the result "a mandala." This, however, cannot be considered the correct usage of the word.

The five buddha families represent the key to the mandala, since the mandala principle relates to each individual as well as to all living beings. At the same time it applies to the directions, elements, colors, shapes, to anything that exists. When categorized, all of these have five aspects. Therefore the principle emerges as the *five* buddha families. That is how it all begins.

To be able to reach this point, a certain amount of preparatory knowledge is needed, as the understanding of the Vajrayana principle is not accessible by drawing a narrow line and saying: "It is always like this." The subject is such that it cannot be pinned down to a definite number of statements and definitions. Within the context of the Vajrayana, everything that needs to be explained and understood is relative. The Buddha said on this point: "I have not said anything." The Vajrayana has a scope that reaches from the most basic explanation up to a field that is beyond verbal expression. Preparation is therefore necessary in order to be able to relate to this subject. We need to develop a state of mind that will not succumb to confusion when facing something that goes beyond our conventional way of thinking.

For this reason the Vajrayana is called "the sacred doctrine" or "the secret doctrine." There is no difference between these as long as they are understood properly.

Otherwise "sacred doctrine" seems preferable since the term "secret" may sound exclusive. In any case, "sacred" should not be misunderstood as prejudice, nor "secret" as implying danger or risk. Both terms signify a simple fact: no one will understand what he or she is unable to understand; each will understand what he or she is able to understand.

According to the Vajrayana we understand in accordance with who we are and with our individual makeup. These teachings are bound by certain rules, and the result will still be an individual understanding. Since these rules were given by the Buddha, there will be his blessing as well.

There is a certain entity or influence that will be activated and will work once it is transmitted and understood properly. This is called the "lineage." Within Vajrayana Buddhism, or Tibetan Buddhism as it is often called nowadays, the significance of the lineage is given prevailing emphasis. If one follows the lineage the chance of proper understanding is far greater, since the lineage contains wisdom and compassion as well as inspiration and knowledge. Without the support of the lineage we have to rely on our ego. Thus the source of our understanding will be the ego. Through the connection with the lineage we overcome this limitation. In the Vajrayana system we are therefore strongly advised to make sure that understanding is approached properly. The traditional way is to learn from the lineage.

Whoever learns from the lineage does not learn from books on shelves, but from great masters like the Karmapa. Whatever such a teacher explains will accord with the original teachings handed down from long ago.

For this reason the subject expressed cannot be just ideas. One has to undergo a thorough process of preparation to be able to speak about or listen to it. In this respect a teacher will feel responsible. This does not mean that the teachings could shatter the mind of a student. If a student derives something useful from them he or she should keep this understanding. Whatever is not understood should just be left alone.

We should not throw the teachings into the garbage; we should burn them. A very common reaction to finding it hard to understand something is to start playing with this non-understanding. We pretend to know, and in that way throw the teachings into the garbage. To burn them means to refrain from this playing and to leave them alone with respect. After some time we may come back to these teachings and find that now we are able to understand.

The principle of the five buddha families encompasses *the five directions,* which are center, east, south, west, and north; *the five materials* of which everything consists, being space, earth, water, fire, and air; and *the five constituents,* which form a person's entire psychological makeup. These constituents are ignorance, desire, anger, jealousy, and ego-pride.

These are the basic factors of the universal law of existence. Without ignorance, desire, anger, jealousy, and pride, a person's psychological system cannot exist. The universe and the body cannot exist without the elements. Without directions, place cannot exist.

These raw materials are the constituents that compose everything that exists. The five buddha families mirror this fivefold principle in its pure aspect. This is the reason why the Buddha taught in this way.

Within the attempt to gain access to this extraordinary and sacred subject of the five buddha families, a certain cultural shock is inevitable. A big leap is required which would overload a person's capacity if it were to be carried out in one go. Therefore a step-by-step process is presented whereby this leap can take place gradually.

To make it briefer, this process can be investigated by means of the five *kleshas* or poisons, which are *ignorance, desire, anger, jealousy, and pride.* On the relative level each has a negative and a positive side. This is quite obvious and easy to understand as far as four of these *kleshas* are concerned. With regard to ignorance, however, some further explanation might be needed. If we do not know what ought to be known we are ignorant in the negative sense, whereas not to know what we should not know is positive ignorance. The borderline between the negative and the positive side of the *kleshas* is as subtle as the fine line between the extremes of genius and insanity.

When we go beyond the positive side of the *kleshas* we are ready for another leap which will result in *wisdom*, the ultimate aspect of desire and so forth. The ultimate face or the essence of the *kleshas* is *five aspects of wisdom*, which manifest as the five buddha families.

To be able to speak of a family there has to be a father, a mother, and at least one child. Although the name "five buddha families" is not altogether perfect, it seems quite appropriate, as the manifestations of the five wisdoms contain a particular fatherly and motherly aspect. In Tibetan these are called *yab* and *yum*, which are the honorific terms for "father" and "mother," and the practitioner is seen as the child.

In short, the father-mother aspect is the manifestation of the five wisdoms. These are the ultimate level of the five positive neuroses, which are one side of a coin. The other side of the coin are the five negative neuroses.

These negative neuroses or *kleshas* always appear together. One cannot describe ignorance unless there is also desire, anger, jealousy, and pride. Neither is it possible to describe desire without ignorance and so forth. They are presented as five due to their different manifestations within different individuals. In some cases all of the five poisons are based on desire; in others they are based on ignorance, pride, jealousy, or anger. The difference lies in the way they condition individuals, but they are always all involved.

The principle of the five buddha families can be shown in many ways. As we have seen, it can be related to the elements, directions, skandhas, and also the five poisons. The latter seems appropriate since every human being has these *kleshas*.

1. *Ignorance*. If, for instance, we do not know what we ought to know, then this is an absolute waste, whereas not to know what should not be known is an absolute gain. This latter expression of ignorance is the extreme opposite, though not contradictory, side of the former.

Its absolute aspect is called the purity of ignorance which is *wisdom vast like space* (Tib. *chö ying ye shé*). This particular term describes the nature of ignorance in its ultimate purity. Since ignorance exists and everyone has it, there must be an ultimate side to it as well. This is "wisdom vast like space." Vastness, or in other words non-existence, is the foundation of everything. Because of non-existence everything exists. Without vastness or space nothing could exist.

The meaning of *chö ying ye shé* is as follows: *Chö* is a word that covers everything that exists. The question often arises whether Buddhism is a religion. People think so, since "-ism" seems to stand for religion. But the teaching of the Buddha has not always been called "Buddhism." It is called the "Dharma" which is the Sanskrit equivalent of *chö*. "Buddhism" is a very new term that came into use in the West about three hundred years ago.

When the Buddha spoke of "Dharma" he spoke of everything that is the subject and object of mind.

The word *ying* has the sense of voidness, vastness, and space. *Chö ying* therefore is "the space of Dharma." *Ye shé* is commonly translated as "wisdom." Literally *ye* means "from the beginning." *Shé* denotes clarity, a sense of togetherness and understanding. *Ye shé* therefore signifies the exposure or the manifestation of truth which is always there. This is translated as "wisdom."

Thus *chö ying ye shé* is clarity, unobscured togetherness, real exposure of the truth which is ever-present, which is the vastness and space of everything that is the subject and object of mind. This is the ultimate aspect of ignorance.

2. *Anger* involves a great amount of ignorance as well as desire, jealousy, and pride. Yet, other than these, it manifests in a specifically active way. Its outcome is very obvious. Someone who is angry will do something. He is likely to scream, break things, or hit another person. Like the other *kleshas*, anger has a negative and a positive side. Anger can provide the mental condition and capacity to get something settled. We are usually able to say "No!" when angry. The negative manifestation of anger is to reject when we ought to accept, whereas it is positive to reject what should be rejected.

The ultimate aspect of anger manifests as a particular wisdom called *mirror-like wisdom.* (Tib. *mé long ta bü ye shé*). In a mirror we see ourselves as we are. In the ultimate sense this implies a certain vividness that enables us to see from inside out. Therefore this wisdom can be described as follows: Everything manifests within voidness. Whatever manifests does so like a reflection, the reflection of interdependence. Every manifestation is nothing but a reflection. This is the particular essence of anger.

In the relative sense, when we are treated with scorn through insulting words or gestures, our anger just comes up. This is called interdependent manifestation. It is a pure reflection. Therefore "mirror-like wisdom" is a very suitable description for the ultimate aspect of anger.

3. In its negative manifestation *ego-pride* causes prejudice. Its positive expression is confidence, which enables us to help both ourselves and others. The deep aspect of ego-pride is a particular wisdom called *wisdom of sameness* or *wisdom of equality* (Tib. *nyam pa nyi kyi ye shé*).

This wisdom illustrates the fact that all sentient beings possess the same ultimate potential. Once this is understood, and we know that everyone has what we have, it is no longer logical to be prejudiced against others. Those who are not carried away by their little knowledge have the feeling of this. The essence of pride is a sense of equality, of oneness. This is wisdom of equality, which can be explained as follows: Every manifestation and that which gives rise to manifestation are just one thing. Due to the presence of the potential there is manifestation. Whatever manifests is the manifestation of the potential or the essence.

These are not different but one. Even oneness is transcended. This is the ultimate aspect of ego-pride.

4. *Desire* is simply making a preference. As long as everything is the same, there is no desire. As soon as one thing is seen to be slightly preferable to another, desire is present. Desire is negative when focused on a harmful object such as the desire to hurt, to get drunk, and so forth. Its positive side is the wish to be a better person, to be helpful to others, and to gain greater knowledge. The ultimate aspect of desire is called *individually cognizing wisdom* (Tib. *so sor tog pa'i ye shé*).

Here, *so sor tog pa* denotes a sense of detail, the absence of haze and confusion. Everything is clear and stands out on its own. One can hardly separate a mixture of milk and water, whereas diamonds and rubies are easily distinguished. The way in which someone who has developed profound awareness and mindfulness will act is an expression of this particular quality.

5. Simply speaking, *jealousy* comes from insecurity and distrust, which may increase up to the point of paranoia. The negative outcome of jealousy is inner insecurity and suspicion. In the positive sense, jealousy will manifest as prudence, which is helpful in many ways. If we are cautious, we run small risk of being trapped in pitfalls that would otherwise prove hard to escape from. A Tibetan proverb says: "The higher we fly the harder we fall. When the wings get numb, better make for the ground."

The ultimate aspect or the essence of jealousy is called the *wisdom of accomplishment* (Tib. *ja wa drub pa'i ye shé*). This might also be expressed as "the job is done." Since everything is ultimately perfect, imperfection does not exist. Nevertheless, on the relative level everything is imperfect.

Perfection, the sense of wholesomeness and together-ness, is the ultimate nature of prudence. Prudence in its turn is the positive aspect of the negative side of jealousy, which manifests as suspicion and paranoia.

The five wisdoms relate to the five *dhyani buddhas* as follows:

(1) Wisdom vast like space relates to Vairochana (Tib. *Nam par nang dzé*),

(2) Mirror-like wisdom to Akshobya (Tib. *Mi kyö pa*),

(3) Wisdom of sameness to Ratnasambhava (Tib. *Rin chen jung den*),

(4) Individually cognizing wisdom to Amitabha (Tib. *Nang wa tha yé*), and

(5) Wisdom of accomplishment to Amoghasiddhi (Tib. *Dön yö drub pa*).

The names given here are those of the fivefold father-aspect, in Tibetan called *yab*. The mother-aspect is the five *yum*, which embody the motherly nature of the five wis-doms. The mother-aspect represents space, and at the same time a sense of gentleness and compassion. The father-aspect represents clarity and skillful means, the aspect of activity. When these are united there is completion.

For this reason the title "buddha families" is used. The original Tibetan term is *gyal wa rig nga*. *Gyal wa* means "glorious." The word *rig* contains a sense of completion which is not hidden but exposed. It denotes complete manifestation which stands out as a family. *Nga* means "five." Thus the phrase is translated as the "five buddha families."

# Glossary

| | |
|---|---|
| bé tsol | bad rtsol |
| chö nyi | chos nyid |
| chö ying ye shé | chos dbyings ye shes |
| dé sheg ka'i la ma | bde gshegs bka'i bla ma |
| Do dé kalpa sangpo | mdo sde skal pa bzang po |
| Dön yö drub pa | don yod grub pa |
| drö | drod |
| dzog pa | rdzogs pa |
| dzog pa chen po | rdzogs pa chen po |
| dzu trül gyi ngön shé | rdzu 'phrul gyi mngon shes |
| gya shung | rgya gzhung |
| gyal wa rig nga | rgyal ba rigs lnga |
| gyü | rgyud |
| jang chub | byang chub |
| jang chub kyi go pang | byang chub kyi go 'phang |

| | |
|---|---|
| jang chub kyi sem | byang chub kyi sems |
| jang chub sem pa | byang chub sems dpa' |
| jang wa | sbyangs ba |
| jar wa | 'byar ba |
| ja wa drub pa'i ye shé | bya ba sgrub pa'i ye shes |
| jing wa | bying ba |
| jor wa | sbyor ba |
| ka | bka' |
| kalpa | skal pa |
| la | bla |
| la ma la chag tsel lo | bla ma la phyag 'tshal lo |
| lhag tong | lhag mthong |
| lo | blo |
| ma | ma |
| ma chö nyug ma | ma bcos gnyug ma |
| mé long ta bü ye shé | me long lta bu'i ye shes |
| men ngag | man ngag |
| Mi kyö pa | mi bskyod pa |
| min pa | smin pa |
| mön lam | smon lam |
| mug pa | rmugs pa |
| nam dag | rnam dag |
| Nam par nang dzé | rnam par snang mdzad |
| Nang wa tha yé | snang ba mtha' yas |

| | |
|---|---|
| ngön shé | mngon shes |
| ngo wo nyi kyi ku | ngo bo nyid kyi sku |
| nö du rung wa | snod du rung ba |
| nyam | nyams |
| nyam pa nyi kyi ye shé | mnyam pa nyid kyi ye shes |
| nyog pa | rnyog pa |
| ö sel wa | od gsal ba |
| Rin chen jung den | rin chen 'byung ldan |
| sab ché | sa bcad |
| sam jor nam dag | bsam sbyor rnam dag |
| sam pa | bsam pa |
| sang gyé | sangs rgyas |
| shen pa | zhen pa |
| shi | bzhi |
| shi né | zhi gnas |
| shing jang wa | zhing sbyangs ba |
| sö me | bzod med |
| sö pa | bzod pa |
| so sor tog pa'i ye shé | so sor rtogs pa'i ye shes |
| sung jug | zung 'jug |
| tog pa | rtogs pa |
| tsé mo | rtse mo |
| tsen dzin | mtshan 'dzin |
| tün gyur | mthun 'gyur |

## Translator's Dedication

Namo Guru
Embodiment of all the Enlightened Ones
In the ten directions and three times,
Please bless us to always see your face,
To receive the nectar of your instruction,
To drink the liquid essence of realization,
To be sustained by the food of compassion
As to no longer be a burden to the world,
But to relieve the burden of all beings
And to be whatever is beneficial to each.

May this book contribute to the removal of all suffering and to the temporary and ultimate welfare and happiness of all sentient beings.

n the United States
nasters